AQA GCSE ENGLISH LANGUAGE AND ENGLISH LITERATURE

TEACHER COMPANION

Adrian Cropper

Peter Ellison

Fran Nantongwe

OXFORD
UNIVERSITY PRESS

Great Clarendon Street, Oxford, OX2 6DP, United Kingdom

Oxford University Press is a department of the University of Oxford. It furthers the University's objective of excellence in research, scholarship, and education by publishing worldwide. Oxford is a registered trademark of Oxford University Press in the UK and in certain other countries

British Library Cataloguing in Publication Data

Data available

ISBN 978-019-834077-5

10 9 8 7 6 5 4 3 2

Printed in Great Britain by Ashford Print and Publishing Services, Gosport

A note on spelling

Certain words, for example 'synthesize' and 'organize', have been spelt with 'ize' throughout this book. It is equally acceptable to spell these words and others with 'ise'.

Contents

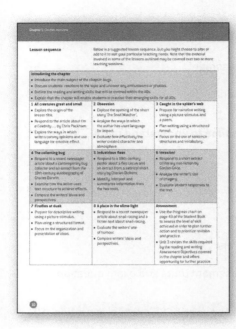

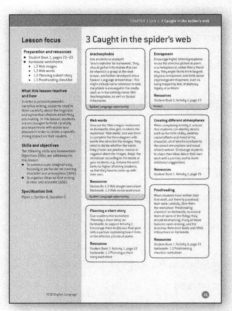

Section 1

Chapter overview

Chapters 1–6 in this Teacher Companion link directly to the corresponding chapters from *Student Book 1: Developing the Skills for Learning and Assessment*. They also aim to provide you with holistic skills and practical support, both for planning and lesson delivery purposes. This starts with looking at the 'why', 'what' and 'how' for the chapter as a whole, and then providing a snapshot medium-term outline. All of the subsequent ideas and guidance reflect the underpinning philosophy of the AQA GCSE English Language resources, allowing you the flexibility to adapt the materials to suit the needs of your students, your department and your teaching style.

Preparing to teach

The Preparing to teach sections in each chapter aim to equip you with useful background to the reading, writing and spoken language skills in focus, linking these with the assessment requirements in the GCSE English Language specification.

Lesson companions

Each 'lesson' in Student Book 1 has a corresponding Lesson Companion in this Teacher Companion. The Lesson Companions open with sharing the 'what' and 'how' for each specific lesson and identifies the specific Skills and Assessment Objectives (AOs) covered and links to the exam papers. The main aim of each Lesson Companion is to provide you with a number of teaching ideas and tips linked to the Student Book activities, some of which relate to resources provided on Kerboodle: Resources and Assessment. The intention is that from these lesson ideas you can create your own lessons, putting a selection of the ideas into a sequence or using some in parallel with different groups of students or individual students in your class. The individual lesson ideas can be used in the way that suits your needs best.

Assessment guidance and answers

Suggestions on how to set up and run the end-of-chapter assessments is provided at the end of chapters 1–6, with sample student responses available on Kerboodle: Resources and Assessment. Answers to Student Book 1 activities, where appropriate, are provided on the final pages of each Teacher Companion chapter.

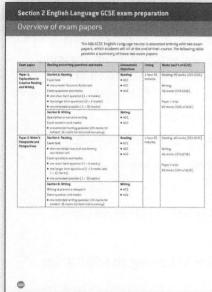

Section 2

Section 2 provides specification information and assessment preparation guidance on the AQA GCSE English Language qualification as well mark scheme and Assessment Objective advice. It also includes elaboration on the materials provided in the AQA GCSE English Language Student Book 2 and links to additional resources on Kerboodle: Resources and Assessment.

Section 3

Section 3 provides information and advice on Spoken Language – the non-examination assessment – and links to additional resources on Kerboodle: Resources and Assessment. Further information is available on the AQA website.

Section 4

Section 4 provides specification information and assessment preparation guidance on the AQA GCSE English Literature qualification. It also includes elaboration on the materials provided in the AQA GCSE English Literature Student Book and links to additional resources on Kerboodle: Resources and Assessment.

Section 5

Section 5 provides planning guidance including questions to consider when planning the course, sample schemes of work and other resources to help you plan and deliver effective GCSE English Language and GCSE English Literature courses and lessons for all your students. The planning resources are also available in an editable format on Kerboodle: Resources and Assessment.

Further AQA GCSE English Language and GCSE English Literature resources

AQA GCSE English Language Student Book 1: Developing the Skills for Learning and Assessment

Approved by AQA, Student Book 1 develops vital reading and writing skills in engaging thematic contexts whilst also focusing on the Assessment Objectives linked to the requirements of the exams. This book is ideal for the start of the GCSE course and features:

- in-depth reading and writing skills development in thematic contexts
- differentiated support and stretch with an embedded focus on technical accuracy
- Assessment Objective focus linked to the requirements of the exams
- opportunities for peer and self-assessment
- regular formative and summative assessments, including sample exam papers.

AQA GCSE English Language Student Book 1: Establishing the Skills for Learning and Assessment

This Student Book focuses on establishing students' reading and writing skills and is ideal for the start of the GCSE course. Structured around engaging themes in the context of the Assessment Objectives, with regular formative and summative assessments, and an embedded focus on SPAG, this book also includes:

- the same core structure as Student Book 1: Developing the Skills for Learning and Assessment
- clear and accessible teaching explanations and source texts
- additional support and steps in the activities
- models of writing with a further focus on basic skills and technical accuracy.

AQA GCSE English Language Student Book 2: Assessment Preparation for Paper 1 and Paper 2

Student Book 2 provides students with all the exam preparation and practice that students need to succeed. The book is divided into Reading and Writing sections (like in the exams) and further divided into chapters which guide students through the questions that they will need to answer in the exam. The book features:

- a range of texts similar to those students will encounter in the exam
- marked sample student responses at different levels
- opportunities for self-assessment and peer-assessment
- advice on how students can improve their responses
- sample exam papers.

AQA GCSE English Literature Student Book

This Student Book provides in-depth skills development for the English Literature specification, including:

- comprehensive coverage and practice of the poetry anthology and unseen poetry requirements

- advice and activities to support Shakespeare, the 19th-century novel and modern prose and drama

- sample student responses at different levels and sample exam-style tasks to help prepare you for the exam paper questions

- Stretch and Support features to ensure all students make progress

- clear, student-friendly explanations of the Assessment Objectives and the skills required to meet them.

AQA GCSE English Language and English Literature Kerboodle: Resources and Assessment

What is Kerboodle?

Kerboodle is a brand-new online subscription-based platform provided by Oxford University Press.

Kerboodle: Resources and Assessment

This AQA GCSE English Language and English Literature Kerboodle: Resources and Assessment provides comprehensive support and resources to enable English departments and individual teachers plan their GCSE courses and deliver effective, personalized lessons that prepare students for the requirements of the exams. Resources include:

- Teaching and learning materials, linked to the corresponding Student Books and Teacher Companion including:

  - Differentiation, personalization and peer/self-assessment worksheets and teaching resources

  - A bank of assignable spelling, punctuation and grammar interactive activities to improve technical accuracy

- Assessment resources including:

  - Marked sample answers and mark schemes

  - Editable versions of the end of chapter Student Book assessments and sample exam papers

- Professional development materials including:

  - Seven specially-commissioned film-based CPD units devised by Geoff Barton with classroom lesson footage, additional interviews and supporting written resources

  - A SPAG guide for GCSE teaching

- Planning resources including:

  - Editable sample schemes of work and medium plans with guidance on what to consider when planning your GCSE course

  - CPD units supporting discussion around departmental GCSE planning

- Digital books including:

  - Student Books 1 (Developing) and 2 and the English Literature Student book in digital format

  - A bank of tools enabling personalization

Chapter overview

Why are we teaching this?

People have always been fascinated by insects. Although they are tiny, they are the most abundant species on Earth. Insects sometimes get a bad press and often provoke strong reactions, but they are essential to our lives. They pollinate our crops, help things decompose and make valuable products, such as honey and silk. The amazing world of insects is still being discovered, and their astonishing creative abilities have given us many of the metaphors by which we describe our own technological advances, such as 'web' and 'cells'.

This chapter uses our natural fascination with insects as the focus for a wide range of reading texts, from fiction by Charles Dickens and Patricia Highsmith to literary non-fiction by Gordon Grice and many contemporary media articles.

As students work though this chapter, they will have the opportunity to develop their reading skills, and in particular to interpret explicit and implicit information from texts. They will also practise their analytical skills by focusing closely on the choices that the writers have made and the effects that they have created for the reader. In addition, students will have the opportunity to create and redraft their own narrative, descriptive and discursive writing in response to visual and textual stimuli.

A range of speaking and listening tasks have been embedded into the lessons and students are encouraged to develop their learning through discussion and collaboration with others.

What are the learning aims?

The main skills and learning objectives are summarized at the start of each lesson in the *AQA GCSE English Language Student Book 1: Developing the Skills for Learning and Assessment*. They are all linked to aspects of the Assessment Objectives (AOs), which are also flagged at the start of each lesson.

By the end of this chapter, students will be developing all of the major skills required by the AQA English Language course. They will be able to:

- read a range of texts closely in order to identify and interpret information and ideas (AO1)
- select and summarize evidence from texts to support a viewpoint (AO1)
- analyse how the writer uses a range of devices and structures for effect (AO2)
- compare writers' ideas and perspectives (AO3)
- evaluate how effectively writers create character, atmosphere and humour (AO4)
- communicate clearly and imaginatively in their own writing (AO5)
- experiment with a range of sentence structures and vocabulary for effect (AO6)
- focus on techniques for spelling and punctuating accurately (AO6).

How will this be assessed?

Activities within each lesson

Teachers can choose to assess some or all of the activities within each lesson. Some activities have been designed to encourage students to work collaboratively; others are designed to encourage students to develop their independent learning skills, and build their reading stamina.

Progress check

The second unit ends with a Progress check (on page 43), which encourages students to reflect on areas of strength and weakness in their learning. This could be completed in collaboration with the teacher or teaching assistant, or with peers, so that students gain a realistic impression of their relative strengths and areas for development. A Progress check is also available on Kerboodle and can be adapted to reflect the breadth of attainment within the class. Ideally, the Progress checks will enable teachers to adapt their teaching in subsequent chapters if areas of weakness have been identified, when the same skills are revisited and developed.

Assessment unit

The assessment unit focuses on the reading and writing skills covered in this chapter, and gives students the opportunity to revise and practise them in a series of activities, using source texts similar to the ones that they will encounter in their exams.

Spoken Language

Teachers will need to offer opportunities for the assessment of Spoken English throughout the course. See pages 122–123 of this Teacher Companion for more information. Activities that could be developed into Spoken Language tasks have been flagged in relevant lessons.

Lesson sequence

Below is a suggested lesson sequence, but you might choose to alter or add to it to suit your particular teaching needs. Note that the material involved in some of the lessons outlined may be covered over two or more teaching sessions.

Introducing the chapter		
• Introduce the main subject of the chapter: bugs.		
• Discuss students' reactions to the topic and uncover any enthusiasms or phobias.		
• Outline the reading and writing skills that will be covered within the AOs.		
• Explain that the chapter will enable students to practise their emerging skills for all AOs.		
1 All creatures great and small	**2 Obsession**	**3 Caught in the spider's web**
• Explore the origin of the lesson title. • Respond to the article about *I'm a Celebrity …* by Chris Packham. • Explore the ways in which writers convey opinions and use language for emotive effect.	• Explore the opening of the short story 'The Snail Watcher'. • Analyse the ways in which the author has used language for impact. • Evaluate how effectively the writer created character and atmosphere.	• Prepare for narrative writing using a picture stimulus and a poem. • Plan writing using a structured format. • Focus on the use of sentence structures and vocabulary.
4 The collecting bug	**5 Industrious fleas**	**6 Invasion!**
• Respond to a recent newspaper article about a contemporary bug collector and an extract from the 19th-century autobiography of Charles Darwin. • Examine how the writer uses text structure to achieve effects. • Compare the writers' ideas and perspectives.	• Respond to a 19th-century poster about a flea circus and an extract from a satirical short story by Charles Dickens. • Identify, interpret and summarize information from the two texts.	• Respond to a short extract of literary non-fiction by Gordon Grice. • Analyse the writer's use of imagery. • Evaluate student responses to the text.
7 Fireflies at dusk	**8 A place in the slime-light**	**Assessment**
• Prepare for descriptive writing using a picture stimulus. • Plan using a structured format. • Focus on the organization and presentation of ideas.	• Respond to a recent newspaper article about snail-racing and a fiction text about snail-racing. • Evaluate the writers' use of humour. • Compare writers' ideas and perspectives.	• Use the Progress chart on page 43 of the Student Book to assess the level of skill achieved in order to plan further action and to prioritize revision and practice. • Unit 3 revises the skills required by the reading and writing Assessment Objectives covered in the chapter and offers opportunity for further practice.

Preparing to teach

Refresh your knowledge

- Some students may be interested to learn more about Patricia Highsmith, a prolific novelist and short-story writer, best known for her psychological thrillers. Students may have come across her work already through films such as *The Talented Mr Ripley* and *Strangers on a Train*. Highsmith was an unusual woman who was known for her many eccentricities. Her work was dark and violent, and sometimes deeply disturbing.

- Some students may not be familiar with Mary Howitt's 1829 poem 'The Spider and the Fly', which is available online. The opening line: '"Will you walk into my parlour?" said the Spider to the Fly' is often quoted (and misquoted) in other works. For example, Howitt's poem was immortalized in the Rolling Stones' song 'The Spider and the Fly'. This aphorism has come to suggest an offer of help which is in fact luring an unwitting victim into a trap. This poem therefore makes an excellent stimulus for a piece of creative writing.

- Flea circuses were a popular attraction in England by the mid-19th century. Real fleas were attached by thin wires to tiny carts and vehicles, and their struggles to free themselves pulled the vehicles along. They were also forced to do other tricks such as walking along tightropes and apparently playing musical instruments, when harnessed by wires. Their great strength relative to their size made them fascinating to watch.

- Dickens' 'The Mudfog Papers', which were written early in his career but published posthumously, contain some examples of the social satire for which Dickens is so well known. The first story 'Public Life of Mr. Tulrumble – Once Mayor of Mudfog' has stood the test of time, while other items are now less well known. The extract about the fleas comes from an item mocking intellectual societies. The story involves the consideration of a paper entitled 'Some remarks on the industrious fleas with considerations on the importance of establishing infant-schools among that numerous class of society...' In this extract, Dickens previews some of the concerns for which his later work is well known, including the creation of ill-advised schemes that claim to benefit the poor.

Links and further reading

- Students who enjoyed Patricia Highsmith's short story might like to try some of her novels, in particular *Strangers on a Train* and *The Talented Mr Ripley*.

- Students with a strong stomach might find Gordon Grice's book on predators interesting: *The Red Hourglass: Lives of the Predators*. It was revised as a new edition in 2010, as part of *Deadly Kingdom: The Book of Dangerous Animals*.

- For a fascinating discussion of the use of insect metaphors in digital culture, direct students towards the work of Jussi Parikka, for instance: http://www.wired.co.uk/news/archive/2013-05/3/insect-technology

- Lesson 5 'Industrious fleas' contains texts about flea circuses. To provide some context for this lesson, show students a short video clip of a genuine flea circus, for example: http://www.britishpathe.com/video/flea-circus

- For students who would enjoy the challenge of Absurdist fiction, direct them towards *The Metamorphosis* by Franz Kafka. First published in German in 1915, the novella tells the tale of a traveling salesman who wakes to find himself transformed into a large insect. The translated text is available online: http://www.online-literature.com/franz-kafka/metamorphosis/1/

- The insect world is fertile ground for proverbs that require some inference. Students might find it interesting to discuss the implications of a selection of the following: http://entnemdept.ifas.ufl.edu/pubs/proverbs.htm

- Articles about insects written for a particular purpose or audience can provide a model for students' own writing, for example: http://www.endangeredspeciesinternational.org/insects8.html

Please note that OUP is not responsible for the third-party content. Although all links were correct at the time of publication, the content and location of this material may change.

Planning guidelines and teaching tips

Think about how you can make the materials relevant to your students and responsive to their particular needs and learning targets. Some suggested approaches to address key areas are provided below.

- In terms of this chapter's themes, all students should find the material accessible. As they start their preparation for GCSE study and beyond, this chapter helps students to understand that one **theme** can be developed across a number of different texts and genres. A wide range of texts has been included in this chapter; however there are opportunities to introduce other relevant fiction and non-fiction texts that relate to the same theme.

- In order to expose students to the idea of using a **picture stimulus** for writing under exam conditions, start collecting a bank of images from different times and cultures. Encourage students to research pictures linked to the theme, and give them the option of using these images for their own writing. Entering a generalized phrase into a search engine, such as 'insects and humans', will yield some interesting images!

- Several **animated films** have been produced on the subject of bugs, some of which the students may have seen, e.g. *Bee Movie* and *A Bug's Life*. Although it may not be the best use of class time to show the whole film, there are scenes that focus on the 'human' characteristics of the insects, and this could stimulate a discussion of vocabulary to describe character traits, and support work on personification and anthropomorphism.

- Make sure that students are not intimidated about sharing their ideas with others and encourage them to **self- and peer-assess** – especially when dealing with imaginative writing. Students will learn from **modelling** – do not be afraid to write in front of students yourself, making mistakes and changing your mind as you work towards a more polished response.

- Some of the extracts in this chapter could create challenges for **more reluctant readers**, as well as **EAL** students. Be prepared to work with these students in one-to-one and guided group contexts to support their reading. Consider strategies to maintain their interest and build their reading stamina, such as quick comprehension quizzes to add an element of competition to their reading.

- Refer to the **Grammar Reference Guide** on Kerboodle for definitions and examples of specific grammatical features covered by this chapter. Students can also be allocated interactive activities to secure their understanding of grammatical concepts and terminology.

- Plan carefully for differentiation, using the **Support and Stretch activities** in the Student Book, and the additional ideas offered in the individual lesson support sections in this Teacher Companion.

Lesson focus

Preparation and resources

- Student Book 1, pages 14–17
- Kerboodle worksheets:
  - 1.1 Identifying information in a blog
  - 1.1 The effect of emotive language
  - 1.1 Writing a response

What this lesson teaches and how

This lesson introduces students to a controversial opinion, expressed through a newspaper article, about the treatment of bugs in a popular TV show. They will identify the explicit information presented in the article, and interpret the implicit information suggested by the writer. They will also start to develop skills for close textual analysis, exploring how emotive language and rhetorical questions are used for effect.

Skills and objectives

The following skills and Assessment Objectives (AOs) are addressed in this lesson:

- To identify and interpret explicit and implicit information and ideas (AO1)
- To analyse how the writer uses rhetorical questions and language for emotive effect (AO2)

Specification link

Paper 2, Section A, Questions 1 and 3

1 All creatures great and small

Writing a blog

You may wish to extend the introductory activity on page 13, by asking students to write a short blog in which they explain their attitude towards bugs. They could include their first encounters with the insect world, the attitudes of their family and friends, or any fears, phobias or particular enthusiasms that they have.

Resources

Student Book 1: Introductory activity, page 13

Identifying information in a blog

As a bridge between the introductory activity and Activity 1 in the lesson, use the worksheet 'Identifying information in a blog' on Kerboodle. This will remind students of the difference between explicit and implicit information.

Resources

Kerboodle: 1.1 Identifying information in a blog worksheet

Intertextual reference

Draw attention to the lesson title. Ask students if they recognize it, and if so from where. (It is the first line of a popular hymn for children and the name of a TV series about a vet.) Challenge students to write down or research the first verse of the hymn. Discuss the message of this verse and how it relates to the newspaper article.

Holding opinions

Play a video clip from *I'm a Celebrity...* in which a contestant eats a living creature during a Bushtucker trial. Put students into groups, and ask each student to explain to the others the circumstances in which they would be prepared to eat a living creature. Finally, choose students who represent different strong opinions to present those opinions to the class.

Resources

Video clip from the Internet

Spoken Language opportunity

The effect of emotive language

Use the worksheet 'The effect of emotive language' on Kerboodle to support students' responses for Activity 3. You could add more quotations and explanations to the grid, depending on the level of support required by your students.

Resources

Student Book 1: Activity 3, page 16
Kerboodle: 1.1 The effect of emotive language worksheet

Writing a response

For students who need additional support to complete Activity 5, use the 'Writing a response' worksheet on Kerboodle. Encourage students to plan the structure of their response carefully, using some of the sentence openers to help them express their observations and ideas.

Resources

Student Book 1: Activity 5, page 17
Kerboodle: 1.1 Writing a response worksheet

Spoken Language opportunity

Lesson focus

Preparation and resources
- Student Book 1, pages 18–21
- Kerboodle worksheets:
  - 1.2 Growing obsession
  - 1.2 Creating horror

What this lesson teaches and how

This lesson focuses on Patricia Highsmith's gripping short story 'The Snail Watcher'. It encourages students to focus on the skills that the writer employs, firstly to hook the reader's interest, and then to develop that interest into a powerful portrayal of one character and his absolute obsession. The steady build-up of atmosphere and tension is monitored, until it develops into a gripping, horrific climax.

Skills and objectives

The following skills and Assessment Objectives (AOs) are addressed in this lesson:
- To evaluate how effectively the writer creates character and atmosphere (AO4)
- To select evidence from the text to support views (AO4)

Specification link

Paper 1, Section A, Question 4

2 Obsession

Powerful story openings

As preparation for the lesson, ask students to bring in a novel that they have enjoyed. Choose a few students to read out the paragraphs that introduce the main character in their book. (This may be the opening paragraphs, but not necessarily.) Discuss briefly what is learnt about the characters. Ask students which introductions they think are most effective, and why.

Analysing language

To support students in responding to Activity 2, give them the worksheet 'Growing obsession' on Kerboodle. You may wish to add more quotations and explanations as models, depending on the level of support that students require.

Resources

Student Book 1: Activity 2, page 20
Kerboodle: 1.2 Growing obsession worksheet

Support

Observing details

Show students a muted clip of the ant sequence from *Indiana Jones and the Crystal Skull* – encouraging them to observe it very carefully. Ask students to write five sentences describing what they saw, conveying the atmosphere and tension as clearly as they can. Students then share their writing in groups. Each group should judge which descriptions were most powerful in creating atmosphere and tension, and share them with the whole class.

Resources

Video clip of ant sequence from *Indiana Jones and the Kingdom of the Crystal Skull* (easily accessible through a search engine)

Creating horror

Give students the worksheet 'Creating horror' on Kerboodle, to help them respond to Activity 4. One example of each detail has been given, but you can adapt this worksheet to give less or more support for differentiation, depending on the needs of your students.

Resources

Student Book 1: Activity 4, page 21
Kerboodle: 1.2 Creating horror worksheet

Patricia Highsmith – author

Higher attaining students could read the complete short story and research more about Patricia Highsmith, who was an unusual woman whose fiction often sprang from her own obsessions. Ask students to discuss whether it is helpful to have biographical details about an author before reading a work of fiction, or whether it may interfere with the reader's response to the text.

Resources

Weblink: http://bookdirtblog.blogspot.co.uk/2013/09/patricia-highsmiths-snail-obsession-and.html

Stretch

Lesson focus

Preparation and resources
- Student Book 1, pages 22–23
- Kerboodle worksheets:
  - 1.3 Web images
  - 1.3 Web words
  - 1.3 Planning a short story
  - 1.3 Proofreading checklist

What this lesson teaches and how

In order to produce powerful narrative writing, students need to think carefully about the linguistic and syntactical choices which they are making. In this lesson, students are encouraged to think carefully and experiment with words and phrases in order to create a specific, strong impact on their readers.

Skills and objectives

The following skills and Assessment Objectives (AOs) are addressed in this lesson:
- To communicate imaginatively, focusing in particular on creating character and atmosphere (AO5)
- To organize ideas so that writing is clear and accurate (AO6)

Specification link

Paper 1, Section B, Question 5

3 Caught in the spider's web

Arachnophobia

Ask students to research 'arachnophobia' for homework. They should gather information that can be shared in a group at the next lesson, and further developed into a Spoken Language presentation. This might include some reference to how the phobia is conveyed in the media, such as in the comedy horror film *Arachnophobia*, as well as factual information.

Spoken Language opportunity

Web words

Give out the 'Web images' worksheet on Kerboodle. Also give students the worksheet 'Web words' and ask them to complete the Venn diagram with words that describe the images. They need to decide whether the words they choose are positive, neutral or negative about the images. Adapt the worksheet according to the needs of your students, e.g. remove the word bank for higher attaining students, so that they have to come up with their own.

Resources
Kerboodle: 1.3 Web images worksheet
Kerboodle: 1.3 Web words worksheet

Spoken Language opportunity

Planning a short story

Give students the worksheet 'Planning a short story' on Kerboodle, to support Activity 1. Encourage them to discuss their plan with a partner, explaining how it links to the stimulus picture or poem.

Resources
Student Book 1: Activity 1, page 22
Kerboodle: 1.3 Planning a short story worksheet

Entrapment

Encourage higher attaining students to use the stimulus picture or poem in a metaphorical, rather than a literal way. They might like to think beyond physical entrapment, and think about psychological entrapment, such as being trapped by fear, or jealousy, loyalty or ambition.

Resources
Student Book 1: Activity 1, page 22

Stretch

Creating different atmospheres

When completing Activity 2, ensure that students can identify details such as the time of day, weather, sound effects and mood of the character, all of which contribute to the overall atmosphere and mood of each extract. Encourage students to share their ideas about their own work with a partner, and to invite additional suggestions.

Resources
Student Book 1: Activity 2, page 23

Proofreading

When students have written their first draft, ask them to proofread their work carefully. Give them the worksheet 'Proofreading checklist' on Kerboodle, to remind them of some of the things they should be checking. If any of these features need revising, use the Grammar Reference Guide and SPAG interactives on Kerboodle.

Resources
Student Book 1: Activity 4, page 23
Kerboodle: 1.3 Proofreading checklist worksheet

4 The collecting bug

Lesson focus

Preparation and resources
- Student Book 1, pages 24–27
- Dictionaries (for each group)
- Kerboodle worksheets:
  - 1.4 Sequencing paragraphs
  - 1.4 Structural features
  - 1.4 Comparing extracts

What this lesson teaches and how

In this lesson, students compare two extracts from different genres and different centuries, but on the same topic of collecting bugs. They will look closely at the way the texts are structured at both paragraph and sentence level. The first extract is from a contemporary newspaper article; the second extract is from a 19th-century autobiography.

Skills and objectives

The following skills and Assessment Objectives (AOs) are addressed in this lesson:
- To examine how the writer uses whole text structure and sentence forms to achieve effects (AO2)
- To compare writers' ideas and perspectives (AO3)

Specification link

Paper 2, Section A, Questions 3 and 4

Collectors

To introduce this lesson, ask students how many of them are collectors, and what they collect. Conduct a quick quiz about the names of collectors and what they collect (e.g. philatelist/stamps; bibliophile/books; palaeontologist/fossils; lepidopterist/butterflies and moths; arctophile/teddy bears; oologist/birds' eggs).

Building vocabulary

After reading through the source text for the first time, ask students to re-read the article in small groups, taking it in turns to read a paragraph. Any unfamiliar words or concepts in the article should be identified and checked with the whole group, e.g. minority view, public image, health hazard, cringe, squirming, salmonella, eradicated, unfairly maligned, exotic, Madagascar. Ensure that dictionaries are available for each group.

Resources
Student Book 1: extract 'The creepy subject of Darren's collecting bug', page 24
One dictionary per group

Sequencing paragraphs

For students who need more help in responding to Activity 1, cut out the summaries on the worksheet 'Sequencing paragraphs' on Kerboodle, so that students can physically re-order them. Tell them to leave a wide gap when the writer changes focus.

Resources
Student Book 1: Activity 1, page 25
Kerboodle: 1.4 Sequencing paragraphs worksheet

Support

Structural features of a text

To support Activity 2, distribute copies of the worksheet 'Structural features' on Kerboodle. Ask students to work in pairs to complete the activity, then to feed back to the whole class. It may be helpful to pre-teach the concepts of 'inside' and 'outside' in this context. The worksheet can be adapted for differentiation, by reducing the number of features for some students.

Resources
Student Book 1: Activity 2, page 25
Kerboodle: 1.4 Structural features worksheet

Sentence forms

If students need further revision about the different types of sentence forms, refer to the Grammar Reference Guide on Kerboodle and give students the relevant interactive activities to work through.

Resources
Student Book 1: Activity 3, page 26

Similarities and differences

Give students the worksheet 'Comparing extracts' on Kerboodle to help them to complete Activity 5. Ensure that they focus sufficiently on the structure and language features, as well as the content of the extracts.

Resources
Student Book 1: Activity 5, page 27
Kerboodle: 1.4 Comparing extracts worksheet

Lesson focus

5 Industrious fleas

Preparation and resources

- Student Book 1, pages 28–31
- Kerboodle worksheets:
  - 1.5 Information about fleas
  - 1.5 Word connotations

What this lesson teaches and how

This lesson is designed to enable students to identify and interpret ideas from 19th-century non-fiction and fiction texts. It focuses on summarizing and synthesizing skills, and will require students to delve beyond the surface meaning of the texts. The texts are an advert from a newspaper, and an extract by Charles Dickens from 'The Mudfog Papers'.

Skills and objectives

The following skills and Assessment Objectives (AOs) are addressed in this lesson:

- To identify and interpret ideas and information (AO1)
- To select and synthesize evidence from different texts (AO1)

Specification links

Paper 1, Section A, Question 1
Paper 2, Section A, Questions 1 and 2*

*Note that in the exam, students will be asked to compare two non-fiction texts in Paper 2, rather than one fiction and one non-fiction.

The Victorian era

It may be necessary to refresh students' knowledge of 19th-century England, to enable them to understand the context of these extracts. Remind them of the effects of the Industrial Revolution, the growing empire, increasing urbanization, growth of factories and industries and population shift towards the towns. Also mention the increasing interest in using animals for entertainment.

Language change

Once students have read the advertisement for Bertolotto's exhibition, draw their attention to the use of capital letters for many noun phrases. Ask them if they know of any languages that still capitalize nouns. For comparative purposes, show them a webpage from a contemporary German newspaper. The British Library website contains some fascinating information about language change. Students could do some research about changes in the English language and develop it into a presentation.

Resources

Student Book 1: Extract of advertisement for Bertolotto's exhibition, page 28
Weblink: http://www.berliner-zeitung.de
Weblink: http://www.bl.uk/learning/langlit/changlang/across/languagetimeline.html

Spoken Language opportunity

Word connotations

When students have read both source texts, ask them to work in pairs to establish which words from the advert had positive connotations, and which words from the story had negative connotations. Use the worksheet 'Word connotations' on Kerboodle to support this analysis of vocabulary. Ask students to explain the reasons for the differences in presentation. Encourage them to think of the writers' different purposes.

Resources

Student Book 1: Source texts on pages 28 and 29
Kerboodle 1.5 Industrious fleas worksheet

Dickens as a social commentator

Activity 3 is designed to stretch higher attaining students. It gives the opportunity to build students' understanding of Victorian England and the concerns of contemporary commentators, such as Charles Dickens. Encourage students to research more into Dickens's campaigns for social reform, for example by using the weblink to the British Library resources below. This could be developed into a Spoken Language presentation.

Resources

Student Book 1: Activity 3, page 31
Weblink: http://www.bl.uk/learning/langlit/dickens/campaigning/social.html

Stretch and Spoken Language

Flea acts

Give students the worksheet 'Information about fleas' on Kerboodle, to help them record their responses to Activity 1. Remind them that when they summarize information, they should always include some quotations to demonstrate the points they make. Emphasize that quotations can be just one or two words, they don't have to be long.

Resources

Student Book 1: Activity 1, page 29
Kerboodle 1.5 Information about fleas worksheet

Lesson focus

Preparation and resources

- Student Book 1, pages 32–35
- Kerboodle worksheets:
  - 1.6 Fans
  - 1.6 Explaining a simile
  - 1.6 More deadly animals

What this lesson teaches and how

Students will be familiar with identifying and discussing the use of imagery in the novels, plays and poetry they have already studied, but this lesson gives them an opportunity to revise what they have learned, and to analyse the same literary techniques that non-fiction writers also use to create powerful effects for the reader.

Skills and objectives

The following skills and Assessment Objectives (AOs) are addressed in this lesson:

- To analyse how the writer uses imagery to achieve effects (AO2)
- To select evidence from the text to support views (AO2)

Specification link

Paper 2, Section A, Question 3

6 Invasion!

Similes and metaphors

If students need reminding of the different techniques used by writers to create imagery, read an image-laden poem such as 'The Ballad of Dick Turpin', by Alfred Noyes, aloud to the group. Ask students to listen for similes and metaphors and note them down afterwards. Discuss why certain images are so powerful. Explain that similes and metaphors are not just used in fiction and poetry.

Resources

Weblink: http://literaryballadarchive.com/PDF/Noyes_2_Dick_Turpin.pdf

Fans

Before they start Activity 1, ask students to write down three different definitions of the word 'fans'. Carry out a quick poll to see which definitions they thought of first. Use the 'Fans' worksheet on Kerboodle to show the image of a Japanese paper fan and an image of a band-winged grasshopper with its wings outstretched. These visuals should help students to explain the effect of the metaphor in the extract.

Resources

Student Book 1: Extract from 'Deadly Animals', page 32
Kerboodle: 1.6 Fans worksheet

Rush hour

In order to draw out the vocabulary needed for Activity 2, show students a clip of passengers squashed in rush-hour trains in the subway of a city such as Tokyo, New York or London. Ask them to describe how they think they would feel. If any of the students use public transport in the rush hour, ask them to describe their experience.

Resources

Student Book 1: Activity 2, page 34

Levels of response

To support students in responding to Activity 2, give out copies of the worksheet 'Explaining a simile' on Kerboodle. The different sized boxes for student comments should give students a sense of the extent to which they need to develop and extend their analysis of words and phrases in order to access higher marks.

Resources

Student Book 1: Activity 2, page 34
Kerboodle: 1.6 Explaining a simile worksheet

More deadly animals

Give higher attaining students the worksheet 'More deadly animals' on Kerboodle. Ask them to read the extract taken from *The Red Hourglass: Lives of the Predators*, and to analyse how Gordon Grice uses language, and imagery in particular, to create a powerful descriptive text for the reader.

Resources

Kerboodle: 1.6 More deadly animals worksheet

Lesson focus

Preparation and resources
- Student Book 1, pages 36–39
- Kerboodle worksheets:
  - 1.7 Image selection
  - 1.7 Questions about images
  - 1.7 Sensory details
  - 1.7 Proofreading checklist

What this lesson teaches and how

In the English Language exam, students will be given a picture as one possible stimulus for their creative writing in Paper 1. Regular exposure to a range of images as an inspiration for creative writing will enable students to tackle this type of question in the exam with confidence.

Skills and objectives

The following skills and Assessment Objectives (AOs) are addressed in this lesson:
- To communicate imaginatively, focusing in particular on description (AO5)
- To organize ideas so that writing is clear and accurate (AO6)

Specification link

Paper 1, Section B, Question 5

7 Fireflies at dusk

Exploring images

Ensure students understand that they will be given an image as one possible stimulus for a creative writing task in their English Language exam. Explain that in order to stimulate ideas, it is often helpful to think about questions in relation to the given images. Use the Kerboodle worksheets 'Image selection' and 'Questions about images' to model and practise this.

Resources

Kerboodle: 1.7 Image selection worksheet
Kerboodle: 1.7 Questions about images worksheet

Sensory details

Give students the worksheet 'Sensory details' on Kerboodle to support their response to Activity 2. Encourage them to think carefully about their choice of vocabulary to describe these sensations, and not just to go for the first words that spring into their minds.

Resources

Student Book 1: Activity 2, page 37
Kerboodle: 1.7 Sensory details worksheet

Support

Fireflies

Some students may be curious about fireflies. Although the main focus of this lesson should be on creative description, you may find it helpful to share some facts about fireflies, to give the photograph some context and background. Use the weblink below to source information about fireflies.

Resources

Student Book 1: Activity 2, page 37
Weblink: http://insects.about.com/od/beetles/a/10-Cool-Facts-About-Fireflies.htm

An unusual viewpoint

Encourage higher attaining students to write their description from an unusual viewpoint, for instance, as a first-person narrative by a firefly! Remind them that the picture should be used to 'suggest' ideas, so they can let their imaginations explore the scene in whatever way they choose.

Stretch

Changing perspectives

When students are planning their descriptions, ensure they understand about how the structure can use different perspectives, for example by zooming in on detail and then expanding out on wider detail, giving a broader perspective. If they have trouble envisaging this concept, look at how this device is used visually in games, such as in the link below.

Resources

Student Book 1: Activity 6, page 39
Weblink: http://www.hiddenobjectgames.com/

Proofreading

When students have written their first draft, ask them to proofread their work carefully. Give them the worksheet 'Proofreading checklist' on Kerboodle, to remind them of some of the things they should be checking. If any of these features need revising, use the Grammar Reference Guide and SPAG interactives on Kerboodle.

Resources

Student Book 1: Activity 8, page 39
Kerboodle: 1.7 Proofreading checklist worksheet

Lesson focus

Preparation and resources
- Student Book 1, pages 40–43
- Kerboodle worksheets:
  - 1.8 Common English idioms
  - 1.8 Exploring meaning
  - 1.8 Comparing texts
  - 1.8 Progress check

What this lesson teaches and how

This lesson is designed to encourage students to think about the flexibility of the English language and the ways in which writers subvert literal meanings to create humour. Students may be more attracted to visual humour in their daily lives, and this lesson enables them to explore verbal humour in more depth. They will also get the chance to compare two texts with a similar theme but different tones.

Skills and objectives

The following skills and Assessment Objectives (AOs) are addressed in this lesson:
- To evaluate how effectively the writer uses humour (AO4)
- To compare writers' ideas and perspectives (AO3)

Specification links

Paper 1, Section A, Question 4*
Paper 2, Section A, Question 4*

*Note that the skills covered in this lesson are relevant to both fiction and non-fiction texts, so they are therefore applicable to both Paper 1 and 2 in the exam. AO3 is tested in Paper 2 (non-fiction) and AO4 is tested in Paper 1 (fiction).

8 A place in the slime-light

Verbal humour

Ask students to discuss what types of media make them laugh. They might consider films, TV shows, radio programmes, video clips on the Internet, etc. Focus on whether students generally find verbal humour more appealing than visual humour. Encourage students to research short clips from the Internet containing clever verbal humour. The Wikipedia page on British Humour contains links to good source material.

Resources
Weblink: http://en.wikipedia.org/wiki/British_humour

Idiomatic language

English humour often relies on a knowledge of idiomatic language, and this can be difficult for non-native speakers to understand. Distribute the survey 'Common English idioms' from Kerboodle and ask pairs of students to complete it, then discuss the non-literal meaning of the idioms. Pairs should feed back to the whole class. Explain that new idioms are constantly evolving, and ask students to be aware of their own use of idiomatic language over the following week.

Resources
Kerboodle: 1.8 Common English idioms worksheet

English village

David Leafe refers to Congham as 'this most English of villages'. Tell the students that they have been asked to contribute images of traditional English villages for an EFL textbook for Spanish children. Ask them to list (or research) ten images that they would include (e.g. the village church, the village green, village school, rural post office/shop, a thatched cottage, cottage garden).

Common meanings

In preparation for Activity 2, distribute the worksheet 'Exploring meaning' on Kerboodle. Ask students to note down in their own words the common meaning of the given words and phrases. When all students have clearly understood the meanings, work through the article focusing on the use of those words in context, and the ways in which the writer has manipulated the original meanings.

Resources
Student Book 1: Activity 2, page 41
Kerboodle: 1.8 Exploring meaning worksheet

Support

Comparing texts

After discussing the texts in Activity 4 in small groups, some students may find it helpful to make brief notes about the similarities and differences between the two texts before attempting Activity 5. Distribute the worksheet 'Comparing texts' on Kerboodle to assist with this. Take feedback and, if necessary, focus on vocabulary to describe tone, which some students may find difficult.

Resources
Student Book 1: Activities 4 and 5, page 43
Kerboodle: 1.8 Comparing texts worksheet

Progress check

Give students copies of the Progress check worksheet on Kerboodle and ask them to evaluate the progress of their skills after studying the texts in the chapter and completing the activities.

Resources
Student Book 1: Progress check, page 43
Kerboodle: 1.8 Progress check worksheet

Unit 3: Assessment

Preparation and resources
- Student Book 1, pages 44–47
- Teacher Companion, pages 107–112 [mark schemes] and 102 [chart showing links between assessment questions and exam paper questions]
- Kerboodle:
  - 1 Assessment
  - 1 Sample responses with examiner's comments

Assessment Objectives

All six reading and writing Assessment Objectives (AOs) are addressed in this unit (AO1, AO2, AO3, AO4, AO5, AO6).

Why do we have an assessment unit?

The final unit in each chapter of *AQA GCSE English Language Student Book 1* focuses on assessment. These units give students an opportunity to practise the skills they have developed throughout the chapter. Regular formal assessments will help to monitor students' progress and assist with target-setting. Some teachers may wish to break down the assessment unit into individual activities or chunks; others may prefer to use the assessment in its entirety, to be completed under exam-type conditions, where the questions are given a set timing.

Many of the activities in this unit build up to assessment questions which echo the tasks that will be set in exam Paper 1 or Paper 2, providing early practice for responding to exam-style questions. A summary of the relationship between the assessment units and exam paper questions can be found on pages 102–103 of this Teacher Companion.

Working through Chapter 1 'Bugs', students will have started to develop some of the essential reading and writing skills for their GCSE exam. This unit will assess whether they have grasped these skills and if they can demonstrate how to employ them in an assessment situation.

What are students demonstrating?

Reading

Students will be able to:
- identify information within a text
- summarize evidence
- analyse how a writer uses language and structure for effect
- evaluate what a writer does to make their writing successful
- compare writers' ideas and perspectives.

Writing

Students will be able to:
- plan, write and proofread a narrative story or description.

How to deliver the assessment

You might wish to separate the reading and writing assessment activities into two separate lessons. Although students will be assessed on their reading and writing together in the exam, as this is their first assessment it may be worth separating the skills to allow them to concentrate on one area only. Look at the questions in all of the activities and, if students are completing these under exam-type conditions, emphasize the importance of time management. A Word document version of the end of chapter assessment is available on Kerboodle which can be assigned to students.

Unit 3: Assessment continued

Understanding the assessment

As this is the first assessment that students have been asked to complete in this book, time should be allocated to discussing what is expected in the assessment activities.

Talk to students about looking carefully at the wording of the questions:

- If they are told to refer to a specific part of the source text, they must ensure that they do focus on that part, and not get distracted by the rest of the text.
- They should note key words used in the questions, such as 'summarize', 'compare', 'explain', 'language', 'structure' and 'character'. Emphasize that these words give a clear indication of what students should be focusing on, and how they should present their response.
- Warn students to check whether the question refers to just one source text or two.
- If the question contains bullet points, students should check that they do cover each point in their response and not just focus on the first one.

Support

Offer support when requested. The aim of the assessment activities is to familiarize students with working in exam-type conditions, with time constraints and precise instructions. It is also to build each student's confidence in preparation for the 'real' exam and to coach students on exam techniques as appropriate.

Marking

Activity 1a can be marked using the suggested answers opposite. This can be done either by teachers or as peer/self-assessment. The longer, more evaluative tasks, for example the 'how' questions, can be marked using the 'Skills descriptors' in the relevant Paper 1 or Paper 2 AQA Specimen mark scheme on pages 107–112 of this Teacher Companion. Sample responses (at Level 3 and Level 4) with examiner comments for Activity 3e are available on Kerboodle.

Use the chart on page 102 of this Teacher Companion to identify which question in the end-of-chapter assessment relates to which exam paper question. If the assessment responses are produced under exam conditions, bear this in mind when marking the assessments. When marking the evaluative responses, you will want to mark using the 'best fit' principle, which means that not all points in the 'Skills descriptors' need to be demonstrated in order to achieve a mark in that level. Nor will those skills necessarily be used consistently throughout the response. Finally, you will need to make a judgement, based on your professional experience and using the AQA sample student responses (available on the AQA website, www. aqa.org.uk), on points such as 'range', 'relevance' and 'accuracy' as used within the 'Skills descriptors' in the mark scheme.

AQA GCSE English Language Student Book 1 answers

Below are the answers to any largely non-subjective *Student Book 1* activities contained within this chapter.

Lesson 1 All creatures great and small
Activity 1

a. Chris Packham has criticized the TV reality show *I'm a Celebrity...*; he hosts BBC2's *Autumnwatch*; he is 48 years old; he found fame when working on *The Really Wild Show*.

b. Chris Packham has high regard for the lives of animals and dislikes people who don't; viewers of *I'm a Celebrity...* are hypocrites, as they value some creatures and not others; Packham is disgusted by the way people are allowed to treat animals on TV; Packham values all living organisms equally.

c. The insects are sometimes eaten alive and can be seen moving; Packham points out that these insects have nervous systems and can feel pain; he insists that their suffering is unnecessary as there are other ways to entertain the same audience.

d. Packham acknowledges that aspects of this TV show are entertaining, such as the physical challenges in which contestants confront fears such as claustrophobia or a fear of going underwater. He notes that 'equally exciting' challenges could be devised without inflicting cruelty on living creatures.

e. This comment suggests that Packham thinks that the people who work on the programme are probably clever, but that they should use their intelligence more responsibly.

Activity 3

a. Language used for emotive effect: slams, cruelty, blasted, appalled, abuse, sickens.

b. Lunatic – uncontrollable 'madness' linked to phases of the moon
Slaughtered – mass destruction linked to the carnage of war

c. Wriggling, shove, starving, exploitation, killing creatures

Activity 4

a. Rhetorical question: 'Surely they have feelings?'

b. Packham is now appealing to the reader's common sense and better nature.

Lesson 2 Obsession
Activity 2

a. He had to check frequently and regularly: 'every hour'; the eggs were his first thought when he woke and the last before he went to sleep; he was excited that another pair of snails was mating – the exclamation mark emphasizes this; he was observing fine details in the eggs, such as the emerging 'miniscule spirals of shells'; his excitement increased as he counted the days; when the first snail hatched from the egg, he felt like a proud father; he felt proud of his rare expert knowledge on the subject of the snails' reproductive cycle; he kept detailed notes on matings and hatchings; he talked obsessively about his findings in social situations to the embarrassment of his wife.

Lesson 4 The collecting bug
Activity 1

a. Correct order: Darren's interest...; Most people...; Darren likes...; An environmental health...; Cockroaches are great...; Cockroaches are actually...; Darren's family...; Darren is about to...

Lesson 5 Industrious fleas
Activity 1

a. Both texts: duelling; dancing; Duke of Wellington; Napoleon Bonaparte
Advert: playing instruments; playing Whist; pulling a bucket
Story: pulling a gig; training for pedestrians

Assessment unit
Activity 1

a. Bed bugs were prevalent in Victorian Britain; they were almost extinct by the 1980s; Rentokil is a pest-control company; infestations of bed bugs have increased by 70 per cent in the last three years; the epidemic looks set to continue.

Chapter 2: Fight for freedom

Chapter overview

Why are we teaching this?

The 19th and 20th centuries saw many struggles for freedom across the globe, and most young people will be aware of the history of those who have fought for freedom from slavery, prejudice and exploitation. However, the global struggle continues into the 21st century, as we see huge numbers of people fleeing from oppressive regimes. Meanwhile, young people in the UK are starting to feel the impact on their freedoms that new technologies and powerful social media are bringing in their wake.

This chapter provides many opportunities for students to explore the wider concept of freedom, as they read and interpret a broad range of texts. Students will have the opportunity to revisit and evaluate some classic texts through close reading, while also gaining a wider perspective about these topics through studying contemporary articles and speeches. In addition, they will have the opportunity to research and communicate their own viewpoints in their own writing.

A range of speaking and listening tasks are embedded into the lessons and students are encouraged to develop their learning through discussion and collaboration with others.

What are the learning aims?

The main skills and learning objectives are summarized at the start of each lesson in *AQA GCSE English Language Student Book 1*. They are all linked to aspects of the Assessment Objectives (AOs), which are also flagged at the start of each lesson.

By the end of this chapter, students will be developing all of the major skills required by the AQA English Language course. They will be able to:

- read a range of texts closely in order to identify and interpret explicit and implicit ideas (AO1)
- select evidence from the text to support a viewpoint (AO1)
- summarize evidence from different texts (AO1)
- analyse how writers use language and structure to achieve effects and influence readers (AO2)
- compare writers' perspectives and how these are conveyed through language and tone (AO3)
- evaluate texts critically and select appropriate evidence from texts (AO4)
- organize information in order to communicate clearly and effectively (AO5)
- communicate imaginatively for different purposes, forms and audiences (AO5)
- check the clarity and accuracy of work (AO6).

How will this be assessed?

Activities within each lesson

Teachers can choose to assess some or all of the activities within each lesson. Some activities have been designed to encourage students to work collaboratively; others are designed to encourage students to develop their independent learning skills and build their reading stamina.

Progress check

The third unit ends with a Progress check (on page 79), which encourages students to reflect on areas of strength and weakness in their learning. This could be completed in collaboration with the teacher or teaching assistant, or with peers, so that students gain a realistic impression of their relative strengths and areas for development. A Progress check is also available on Kerboodle and can be adapted to reflect the breadth of attainment within the class. Ideally, these Progress checks will enable teachers to adapt their teaching in subsequent chapters if areas of weakness have been identified, when the same skills are revisited and developed.

Assessment unit

The assessment unit focuses on the reading and writing skills covered in this chapter, and gives students the opportunity to revise and practise them in a series of activities, using source texts similar to the ones they will encounter in their exams.

Spoken Language

Teachers will need to offer opportunities for the assessment of Spoken English throughout the course. See pages 122–123 of this Teacher Companion for more information. Activities that could be developed into Spoken Language tasks have been flagged in each lesson.

Lesson sequence

Below is a suggested lesson sequence, but you might choose to alter or add to it to suit your particular teaching needs. Note that the material involved in some of the lessons outlined may be covered over two or more teaching sessions.

Introducing the chapter

- Introduce the main subject of the chapter: freedom.
- Discuss students' reactions to the topic and establish which relevant texts they have already read or heard, e.g. Martin Luther King's speech.
- Outline the reading and writing skills that will be covered within the AOs.
- Explain that the chapter will enable students to practise their emerging skills for all AOs.

1 Written in black and white	2 Sugar and spice	3 Speaking out
• Explore the origin of the lesson title. • Explore a famous speech by Martin Luther King, an extract from Andrea Levy's novel *Small Island* and an anti-imperialist article by Benjamin Zephaniah. • Select and interpret implicit and explicit information from the texts.	• Explore the origin of the lesson title. • Analyse the fictional extract from an essay by Virginia Woolf and two post-war texts on gender. • Continue to interpret writers' ideas. • Start to compare ideas and tone.	• Prepare for writing a viewpoint after conducting some individual research. • Plan writing using a structured format. • Focus on the clarity and accuracy of writing.
4 Big Brother	**5 A slave's tale**	**6 Soup and crackers**
• Respond to the opening extract from *Nineteen Eighty-Four* by George Orwell and an extract from Malala Yousafzai's autobiography. • Analyse how the writers use language and structure to achieve effects. • Compare the writers' ideas and perspectives.	• Explore an extract from the 19th-century autobiographical text: *Incidents in the Life of a Slave Girl*. • Select and analyse evidence from the text. • Write an imaginative first-person narrative.	• Respond to a 19th-century report about poverty in London, and a 21st-century article about poverty. • Compare the writers' perspectives and how these are conveyed. • Evaluate the texts critically.
7 Fighting talk	**8 Operation Dynamo**	**Assessment**
• Respond to an autobiographical account of a soldier in the First World War and 'A Soldier's Declaration' by Siegfried Sassoon. • Analyse how the writers use language and tone to influence their readers.	• Respond to an eye-witness account of the evacuation of Dunkirk. • Analyse the writer's use of structure by storyboarding the account. • Critically evaluate the text, and students' responses to it.	• Use the Progress chart on page 79 of the Student Book to assess the level of skill achieved in order to plan further action and to prioritize revision and practice. • Unit 4 revises the skills required by the reading and writing Assessment Objectives covered in the chapter and offers opportunity for further practice.

Preparing to teach

Refresh your knowledge

- You may need to remind students that Dr Martin Luther King was a Baptist minister and civil rights activist, probably best remembered today for his 'I Have a Dream' speech, which he gave at a civil rights rally in Washington in 1963. The rally demanded an end to racial discrimination in the USA and the enactment of meaningful civil rights legislation. In 1964, King received the Nobel Peace Prize for challenging racial inequality through non-violence. The night before he was assassinated in Memphis, King addressed a rally and delivered his 'I've Been to the Mountaintop' address at Mason Temple. The last eight minutes of this speech, from 'You know, several years ago, I was in New York City...' is worth sharing with students if they haven't heard it: http://www.americanrhetoric.com/speeches/mlkivebeentothemountaintop.htm

- Andrea Levy is a British author, born in London in 1956. Her parents came to the UK from Jamaica on the *Empire Windrush* in 1948. Levy started writing in her mid-30s at a time when there was little fiction based on the experience of Jamaicans living in London. Levy's novels reflect the experiences of the British-born black Londoners who were struggling to negotiate challenges to their racial and cultural identity in the mid-20th century. Her most highly acclaimed novel, *Small Island*, written in 2004, has won several prestigious literary prizes.

- Some students will already be familiar with the work of Benjamin Zephaniah, particularly through poetry anthologies such as *Talking Turkeys* and *School's Out*. Zephaniah was expelled from school at the age of 13, after struggling with literacy. He has claimed that his mission was to take his poetry to people who did 'not read books'.

Zephaniah has spoken out about a range of issues, including homophobia in Jamaica, special needs education, the disestablishment of the British monarchy and veganism. His refusal to accept an OBE in 2003 attracted a lot of attention. Zephaniah has received a number of prestigious prizes, and been awarded several honorary university doctorates. He was listed at number 48 in *The Times*' list of 50 greatest post-war writers.

- In 2006, The Declaration of Montreal demanded that all states recognize May 17th as the International Day Against Homophobia. This date is now celebrated in many states, particularly in Europe and Latin America. Over the last few years in the UK there has been growing pressure to expose and challenge homophobia within schools and workplaces, and the campaign is now starting to focus on homophobia within sport. In September 2014, supported by celebrities, several high-profile professional footballers wore rainbow laces in their boots to draw attention to Stonewall's Rainbow Laces campaign, which supports kicking homophobia out of football.

- *Nineteen Eighty-Four* is a work of fiction written by the novelist George Orwell in 1948. The story is set in a dystopian state in which individualism and independent thought are sacrificed to the desire of the state to maintain total control over its citizens. The citizens cannot escape from the all-seeing 'eye' of the Party Leader, and even their 'thoughtcrimes' are punished. This classic novel serves as an introduction to the tyranny of totalitarianism, and many students will recognize concepts such as 'Big Brother', 'Room 101' and 'doublethink'.

- Social researcher Henry Mayhew is best known for the groundbreaking work he carried out in the mid-19th century about the lives of London's poorest citizens. His book *London Labour and the London Poor* was published in 1851 and had some impact on the formation of social policy in the second half of the century. Mayhew's detailed descriptions of the urban poor were said to have influenced the portrayal of some of Dickens' best-loved characters.

Links and further reading

- Before starting this chapter, direct students towards the work of the United Nations in championing the rights of children around the world. The articles of the UN Convention on the Rights of the Child provide a useful framework for the discussion of rights and freedoms: http://www.unicef.org.uk/UNICEFs-Work/UN-Convention/

- It may be helpful to display the following 'child-friendly' summary in the classroom: http://www.unicef.org.uk/Documents/Publications/Child_friendly_CRC_summary_final.pdf

- For students who are interested in the struggle for freedom from slavery, the following website provides some powerful personal accounts: http://atlantablackstar.com/2014/07/06/our-stories-10-powerful-slave-narratives-worth-reading/3/

- The following website gives the lyrics of a rap poem entitled 'This is black history', which challenges the approach often taken in UK schools and provides a lot of references for students to follow up: http://www.beatknowledge.org/2011/10/03/this-is-black-history-video-and-lyrics/

- For a challenging but fascinating article about Nelson Mandela, and the way in which black history has often been sanitized, direct students towards Musa Okwonga's speech to the Edinburgh University Students' Union: http://www.okwonga.com/beware-the-black-sainthood-my-speech-at-edinburgh-universitys-student-union/

- Many organizations that campaign for the freedoms of those around the world provide a range of educational resources for young people. Some examples are: http://www.amnesty.org/en/human-rights-education/resources; http://www.srtrc.org/shop/index.php?main_page=index&cPath=4; http://www.actionaid.org.uk/school-resources; http://www.stonewall.org.uk/at_school/education_for_all/quick_links/education_resources/secondary_school_resources/

- Students who haven't already encountered Benjamin Zephaniah's prose may enjoy the following novels: *Face*, *Refugee Boy*, *Gangsta Rap* and *Teacher's Dead*. Students may also be interested and challenged to read some of Zephaniah's political poems, including the powerful 'What Stephen Lawrence Has Taught Us'.

- For wider reading about the First World War, popular novels about this era include *Birdsong* by Sebastian Faulks and *A Farewell to Arms* by Ernest Hemingway. The novel *All Quiet on the Western Front* is also set in this era, with the story told from the German viewpoint. For less confident readers, *War Horse* by Michael Morpurgo provides a useful introduction to this period of history. The poetry anthology, *Scars upon my Heart*, edited by Catherine Reilly, presents a series of poems depicting the experience of a wide range of women during the war.

Please note that OUP is not responsible for the third-party content. Although all links were correct at the time of publication, the content and location of this material may change.

Planning guidelines and teaching tips

Think about how you can make the materials relevant to your students and responsive to their particular needs and learning targets. Some suggested approaches to address key areas are provided below.

- For some students, there are themes in this chapter that may need to be handled sensitively, for example **homophobia, racial and gender discrimination, mental health issues**. Teachers will need to use their professional judgement and knowledge of the class when selecting resources and activities for their group. It may also be helpful to plan this unit carefully as a department, drawing on the skills and experiences of colleagues.

- Some of the topics covered in this chapter are areas of **current debate** and development. Organizations that produce updated information can provide additional resources for use in class. Many of these organizations are active on online social networks; encourage students to follow organizations that provide information about the topics they are studying.

- There are many short texts — both fiction and non-fiction — on topics of contemporary interest, published in books and magazines. If possible, ask your librarian to produce a book box of short reads to **engage more reluctant readers** and build subject vocabulary. Give students opportunities to read for a few minutes in class each week, and talk about their reading with their peers.

- Many of the topics covered in this chapter involve people with courage speaking out in front of people who do not share their viewpoint. Encourage students to make their voices heard. **Videoing and audio-recording** discussions and presentations can actually protect students from fear of inappropriate peer feedback.

- Use carefully selected **images** whenever possible to support and inspire discussion about sensitive and controversial themes, such as slavery. For example, the website of the Underwater Sculpture Park in Grenada provides some powerful images.

- Encourage students to make links between their reading of **historical literary texts and current developments**. For example, students may have heard about or visited the 'Blood Swept Lands and Seas of Red memorial' in Autumn 2014, but also be interested to learn that a luxury meal for arms dealers was held in the Tower of London a few days later. Some students may be able to link this dichotomy to their reading of Sassoon's 'Declaration'.

- Refer to the **Grammar Reference Guide** on Kerboodle for definitions and examples of specific grammatical features covered by this chapter.

- Plan carefully for differentiation, using the **Support and Stretch activities** in the Student Book, and the additional ideas offered in the individual lesson support sections in this Teacher Companion.

Lesson focus

Preparation and resources

- Student Book 1, pages 50–53
- Kerboodle worksheets:
  - 2.1 Freedom quotations
  - 2.1 Explicit ideas
  - 2.1 Implicit ideas – true or false?

What this lesson teaches and how

This lesson gives students the opportunity to draw out explicit and implicit ideas from a variety of texts, all linked by the theme of racial prejudice. Extracts include a speech by Martin Luther King, the novel *Small Island* by Andrea Levy, and an article by Benjamin Zephaniah. Students are encouraged to blend quotations into their responses.

Skills and objectives

The following skills and Assessment Objectives (AOs) are addressed in this lesson:

- To identify and interpret explicit and implicit ideas (AO1)
- To select evidence from texts (AO1)

Specification links

Paper 1, Section A, Question 1*
Paper 2, Section A, Question 1*

*The skills taught in this lesson are relevant to both exam papers, because they are transferable between fiction and non-fiction texts.

1 Written in black and white

What is freedom?

To add challenge to the introductory activity of discussing the quotations about freedom printed on page 49 of the Student Book, give students the worksheet 'Freedom quotations' on Kerboodle to complete and discuss.

Resources

Student Book 1: Activity a, page 49
Kerboodle: 2.1 Freedom quotations worksheet

Stretch

Justice rolls down

Point out that King uses a biblical reference in his speech, 'until justice rolls down like waters…' (Old Testament, Amos, Chapter 5, verse 23). Encourage students to discuss why King uses this reference. Draw out that he was an American pastor, and many in his audience would have been familiar with biblical texts. Focus on the impact of this imagery and the potential effect on the audience.

Resources

Student Book 1: King's speech, page 50
Bible, Amos, Chapter 5, verse 23

Explicit ideas

Distribute the worksheet 'Explicit ideas' on Kerboodle and encourage students to find the shortest possible quotation from the text which supports each idea.
This worksheet could be extended or simplified, depending on students' needs. Use the starter paragraph for students who need support, but then encourage them to write independently if they can.

Resources

Student Book 1: Activities 1 and 2, page 51
Kerboodle: 2.1 Explicit ideas worksheet

Support

Andrea Levy

You might want to give students some background about the author (or ask them to research it themselves). Levy's parents were migrants from Jamaica who sailed to England on the *Empire Windrush* in 1948. Encourage students to read more of Levy's work and to discuss how her background and personal experiences are reflected in her novels.

Resources

Student Book 1: Activity 4, page 53

Implicit ideas – true or false?

Some students may benefit from completing the worksheet 'Implicit ideas – true or false?' on Kerboodle before tackling Activity 4 in the Student Book. Ask students to read through the statements in pairs, marking whether they are true or false. Remind them that they need to be able to justify their decisions. (The answers are T, T, F, F, F, T, F, T, T.) Discuss any statements they were unsure about.

Resources

Student Book 1: Activity 4, page 53
Kerboodle: 2.1 Implicit ideas – true or false? worksheet

Support

Honours

Explain that the OBE is awarded for 'valuable service' to the arts and sciences, public services and charitable organizations of all kinds in the UK. The motto associated with the medal is 'For God and the Empire'. Place students in groups and ask them to discuss whether honours are still appropriate in 21st-century Britain and, if so, who should be honoured?

Lesson focus

Preparation and resources
- Student Book 1, pages 54–57
- Kerboodle worksheets:
  - 2.2 Shakespeare's sister
  - 2.2 A woman's job

What this lesson teaches and how

This lesson is designed to extend students' ability to identify and interpret explicit and implicit ideas in more challenging texts. Looking at a text by Virginia Woolf, a radio script from 1947, and a contemporary newspaper article, students will be encouraged to interpret ideas (some of which are controversial) suggested by the writers. They will also start to link and compare ideas and tone.

Skills and objectives

The following skills and Assessment Objectives (AOs) are addressed in this lesson:
- To interpret explicit and implicit ideas (AO1)
- To begin to compare ideas and tone (AO3)

Specification links

Paper 1, Section A, Question 1
Paper 2, Section A, Question 4*

*Note that the skills of comparing texts (AO3) will only be tested in Paper 2, but these skills are relevant to both fiction and non-fiction texts.

2 Sugar and spice

Choices

Read the introductory paragraph with the class. Encourage discussion. Ask: Are the statements true for all young people in the UK? Are the 'choices' identified in the text available to young people from all backgrounds and cultures? Encourage students to consider whether all young people benefit equally from these 'choices' nowadays.

Resources

Student Book 1: page 54

Shakespeare's sister

For students who need more support, give out copies of the worksheet 'Shakespeare's sister' on Kerboodle. After cutting out the statements, students should put them into the correct sequence. Note that some statements contain interpretations of the text. Discuss whether Judith had any other options than to take her own life. For further exploration of the theme of women's options, historically, share the poem 'Cousin Kate', by Christina Rossetti, with the class.

Resources

Student Book 1: Activity 1, page 55
Kerboodle: 2.2 Shakespeare's sister worksheet
Weblink: http://www.poetry-archive.com/r/cousin_kate.html

Support

A woman's job

Revise students' understanding of the difference between implicit and explicit information in texts by using the worksheet 'A woman's job' on Kerboodle. Discuss students' responses. Challenge higher attainers to write a couple of paragraphs about how relevant this picture of family life is nowadays. Encourage them to consider issues such as different types of families, values and attitudes, beyond just housework.

Resources

Student Book 1: Activity 4, page 56
Kerboodle: 2.2 A woman's job worksheet

Who are we?

Ask students to focus on the pronouns in the *Woman's Hour* script. For example, who are 'they' in the first sentence? Who are 'we' ('we're' and 'we've') in the same paragraph? Encourage students to discuss the effect of using third- and first-person pronouns in the plural in this context. Draw out the sense of camaraderie created by the use of 'I' and 'we'.

Resources

Student Book 1: source text, page 56

Stretch and SPAG

21st-century choices

Activity 3 could be extended into a research activity, and then a Spoken Language presentation about the constraints that still face some young women in the UK, and in many other parts of the world. Explain that the United Nations declared that October 11th each year would be the International Day of the Girl. Draw attention to the work of young women such as Emma Watson and Malala Yousafzai who have spoken openly about girls' education and choices.

Resources

Student Book 1: Activity 3, page 55
Weblinks: http://www.unwomen.org/en/news/stories/2014/9/emma-watson-gender-equality-is-your-issue-too
http://mic.com/articles/101072/8-ways-malala-has-made-the-world-better-for-women

Spoken Language opportunity

Lesson focus

Preparation and resources
- Student Book 1, pages 58–59
- Kerboodle worksheets:
  - 2.3 Prejudice in football
  - 2.3 Checklist of features

What this lesson teaches and how

This lesson gives students the opportunity to research a topic of contemporary significance, then organize and communicate their views on that topic clearly and effectively. They are also encouraged to practise their proofreading and editing skills.

Skills and objectives

The following skills and Assessment Objectives (AOs) are addressed in this lesson:
- To organize information in order to communicate clearly and effectively (AO5)
- To check the clarity and accuracy of their work (AO6)

Specification link

Paper 2, Section B, Question 5

3 Speaking out

Prejudice mind map

As prejudice is a sensitive topic, give students time in small groups to discuss the different types of prejudice that exist in the 21st century. Ask them to produce a mind map of ideas within their group, and remind them that all suggestions should be accepted at this stage. Encourage a volunteer to feed back ideas to the whole class. Be aware that this may be a difficult topic for some students.

Prejudice on the terraces

Before reading the source text, ask if any students have witnessed prejudiced comments of any kind at football matches. For example, some students may know of incidents that led to fans reporting abuse at a nearby stadium. Before tackling Activity 1, provide students with some background information about the work of 'Show Racism the Red Card' and 'Stonewall': two organizations that produce a range of classroom resources.

Resources

Weblink: http://www.srtrc.org/ educational/teachers-area/ homehttp://www.stonewall.org.uk/

Anti-gay abuse in football

Some students may benefit from completing the worksheet 'Prejudice in football' on Kerboodle, to support their understanding of the source text. This will also help to widen their vocabulary and refresh their knowledge of some basic grammatical terms. If necessary, assign specific SPAG interactives to students to revise their knowledge.

Resources

Student Book 1: source text, page 58
Kerboodle: 2.3 Prejudice in football worksheet

Support and SPAG

Research

Be aware of students' sensitivities towards some issues, such as obesity. Encourage them to choose examples of prejudice that they feel comfortable with exploring and talking about. However, do point out the similarities between many forms of prejudice.

Resources

Student Book 1: Activity 2, page 59
Weblinks: http://www.theguardian. com/commentisfree/2014/jul/13/ overweight-people-help-malice- gastric-bands-nhs
http://www.huffingtonpost. co.uk/tim-farron/rainbow-laces- campaign_b_5789518.html

Promoting diversity

Ask students to work in groups to create a poster that celebrates and promotes diversity in the UK in the 21st century. For example, each group could choose at least ten images of well-known figures from a variety of backgrounds who have made a positive contribution to life in the UK. Encourage one person from each group to present their poster, explaining the choices.

Checklist of features

If necessary, give students the worksheet 'Checklist of features' on Kerboodle, to help them assess their own work, or that of their peers. Note that this should be used as part of a work-in-progress stage, rather than any sort of marking scheme. These prompts could be adapted to many different writing tasks and expanded to suit the needs of your students.

Resources

Student Book 1: Activity 2, page 59
Kerboodle: 2.3 Checklist of features worksheet

Lesson focus

4 Big Brother

Preparation and resources
- Student Book 1, pages 60–65
- Kerboodle worksheets:
  - 2.4 Opening lines
  - 2.4 *I am Malala*

What this lesson teaches and how

This lesson is designed to explore the ways in which writers use language and structure to create specific effects for the reader. Using extracts from the novel *Nineteen Eighty-Four* by George Orwell, and Malala Yousafzai's autobiography, *I am Malala*, students will compare the ways in which writers convey their perspectives using language and structure.

Skills and objectives

The following skills and Assessment Objectives (AOs) are addressed in this lesson:
- To analyse how writers use language and structure to achieve effects (AO2)
- To compare how writers convey their perspectives using language and structure (AO3)

Specification links

Paper 1, Section A, Question 2
Paper 2, Section A, Question 4*

*Note that students will only need to compare texts in Paper 2, where they will compare two non-fiction texts. However, these skills are transferable between fiction and non-fiction texts.

Opening lines

Give students the worksheet 'Opening lines' on Kerboodle. Even if students do not know the novels, encourage discussion of the possible genre, century and plot of the quotations. Draw out the importance of opening lines to catch the interest of the reader and set the scene. (Answers: A = *Rebecca*, B = *Pride and Prejudice*, C = *Harry Potter*, D = *Lord of the Flies*, E = *Middlemarch*, F = *Frankenstein*, G = *Twilight*, H = *Brighton Rock*, I = *The Hunger Games*, J = *David Copperfield*)

Resources
Kerboodle: 2.4 Opening lines worksheet

Connotation

If students need a reminder of the concept of 'connotation', write three words on the board, e.g. spiders, football, festival. Ask them to jot down one word or phrase only in response to each of the three. Share the ideas, drawing attention to the reasons why responses may differ, depending on individual associations.

Support

Dystopia

Write 'dystopia' on the board and invite definitions. Discuss, clarifying meaning. Before students tackle Activity 4, project an image depicting a futuristic dystopian city (suggestion below). Ask students to work in pairs and list words and phrases that the image suggests. Feed the ideas back to the class. Encourage students to widen their vocabulary, and not just use the first words that come into their heads.

Resources
Weblink: http://www.pbase.com/yammering_splat_vector/image/133751186

Shifts in structural focus

To assist students with Activity 7, distribute the worksheet '*I am Malala*' on Kerboodle. This leads students through each paragraph, giving an opportunity for them to make notes on each one, considering aspects of character, setting and viewpoint.

Resources
Student Book 1: Activity 7, page 65
Kerboodle: 2.4 *I am Malala* worksheet

Support

Planning comparisons

Before tackling Activity 9, encourage students to discuss the similarities and differences between the two texts. They might then find it helpful to plan their response as a Venn diagram, showing where similar ideas and techniques overlap. Remind students to consider both language and structure in their response.

Resources
Student Book 1: Activity 9, page 65

Film directions

Give students another extract to read (of your choice) and ask them to make notes for a camera person, showing the different perspectives and structure for the film. They should be able to describe the focus, the camera sweeps, the changing perspectives and lens filters, in order to create specific effects for the viewers. This activity will reinforce students' understanding of 'structure' in a written work.

Stretch

Lesson focus

Preparation and resources
- Student Book 1, pages 66–67
- Kerboodle worksheets:
  - 2.5 Life of a slave girl
  - 2.5 Notes for a narrative
  - 2.5 Opening paragraphs

What this lesson teaches and how

This lesson focuses on an extract from the autobiographical account by Harriet Ann Jacobs: *Incidents in the Life of a Slave Girl*. Students will look in particular at the effectiveness of a first-person narrative in creating a strong impact on the reader. The extract is used as a springboard for students' own narrative writing.

Skills and objectives

The following skills and Assessment Objectives (AOs) are addressed in this lesson:
- To select evidence from texts (AO1)
- To communicate imaginatively for different purposes, forms and audiences (AO5)

Specification links

Paper 1, Section B, Question 5
Paper 2, Section A, Question 1

The reading and writing skills in this lesson are transferable between fiction and non-fiction texts.

5 A slave's tale

Moving here

Before starting this lesson, ask students to research people who have written a first-person narrative account of moving away from their home in difficult circumstances. They should identify three different people and note down where they moved from and why. If necessary, direct them to the websites below.

Resources

Weblinks: http://webarchive.nationalarchives.gov.uk/+/http://www.movinghere.org.uk/stories/default.asp
http://www.refugee-action.org.uk/assets/0000/7170/MMM_pdf.pdf

Human Rights

As background to the issue of child slavery, explain that in 1989, governments worldwide adopted the UN Convention on the Rights of the Child. Ask students to work in groups and list ten rights which they think every child in the world is entitled to. Feed back to the class. Distribute an overview summary of the UNCRC articles (see link below). Draw students' attention to Article 35, on the subject of Human Trafficking.

Resources

Weblink: http://www.unicef.org/crc/files/Rights_overview.pdf

Pronouns

To support students with Activity 2a, distribute the worksheet 'Life of a Slave Girl' on Kerboodle. Ask students to highlight all the pronouns which indicate a first-person narrator.

Resources

Student Book 1: Activity 2a, page 67
Kerboodle: 2.5 Life of a Slave Girl worksheet

Support and SPAG

Creating a persona

Before students start Activity 2b, ask them to work in pairs and choose three characters, one each from the 19th, 20th and 21st centuries, who would make an interesting persona for a story. Encourage them to link into other areas of the curriculum, e.g. a scientist searching for a cure for malaria or a suffragette campaigning for the vote.

Resources

Student Book 1: Activity 2b, page 67

Challenge

Planning a narrative

To help students plan their narrative writing, distribute the worksheet 'Notes for a narrative' on Kerboodle. If students need a basic storyline, you could refer them to the story 'Chaga and the Chocolate Factory' from the Stop the Traffik website. (The story is aimed at younger children, but could still be the basis of students' own first-person narratives, in the voice of Chaga.)

Resources

Student Book 1: Activity 2b, page 67
Kerboodle: 2.5 Notes for a narrative worksheet
Weblink: http://www.stopthetraffik.org/campaign/chocolate/what-you-can-do/16

Opening paragraphs

To support students who struggle to start their own writing, distribute the 'Opening paragraphs' worksheet on Kerboodle. They should choose one of the two personae – the bully or the bullied – to narrate the incident.

Resources

Student Book 1: Activity 2b, page 67
Kerboodle: 2.5 Opening paragraphs worksheet

Support

Lesson focus

6 Soup and crackers

Preparation and resources
- Student Book 1, pages 68–71
- Kerboodle worksheets:
  - 2.6 Signposted reading
  - 2.6 Sentence forms
  - 2.6 Language and effect

What this lesson teaches and how

This lesson enables students to compare the ways in which different writers convey information and perspectives on the same topic. They will start to learn how to evaluate texts, giving their personal response.

Skills and objectives

The following skills and Assessment Objectives (AOs) are addressed in this lesson:
- To synthesize evidence from different texts (AO1)
- To compare writers' perspectives and how these are conveyed (AO3)
- To evaluate texts critically (AO4)

Specification links

Paper 1, Section A, Question 4*
Paper 2, Section A, Questions 2 and 4*

*Note that comparison (AO3) is a skill required in Paper 2, and evaluation (AO4) is a skill required in Paper 1. These skills are transferable between fiction and non-fiction texts.

Need or want?
Before starting this lesson, ask students to make a list of material possessions that they could not live without in their daily lives. Take feedback as a class. Clarify the difference between 'need' and 'want'.

Who will buy?
Before reading the source text about the costermongers, show the class a clip of the song 'Who will buy?' from Lionel Bart's 1968 film adaptation of the musical show *Oliver*. This romanticized view of the costermongers' life will be challenged by Mayhew's text.

Signposted reading
Distribute the worksheet 'Signposted reading' on Kerboodle, before students read the source texts. Ask them to read the headings carefully so that they will focus on the key organizing topics when reading the texts. Explain that having 'signposts' before reading can help to process the content of unfamiliar texts. This is particularly the case when preparing to summarize and compare texts. Students could then work in pairs to find relevant quotations and compare their choices with another pair.

Resources
Student Book 1: Activity 1a, page 70
Kerboodle: 2.6 Signposted reading worksheet

Support

Sentence forms
Refresh students' knowledge of how to use appropriate sentence forms when comparing information. Use the worksheet 'Sentence forms' on Kerboodle to illustrate a variety of possibilities. Encourage students to experiment with using different sentence forms, and a variety of suitable punctuation in their own writing.

Resources
Student Book 1: Activity 1c, page 70
Kerboodle: 2.6 Sentence forms worksheet

SPAG

Language and effect
Before students start choosing their own quotations for Activity 3, distribute the worksheet 'Language and effect' on Kerboodle. After completing the grid, ask students to choose more quotations of their own and explain what particular effects the language created for them as readers. If they need help, suggest they look at the direct speech and colloquial expressions in Soup and crackers, and the more formal, sophisticated language in the *London Poor* extract, e.g. 'fully occupied', 'ensure her a safe reception'.

Resources
Kerboodle: 2.6 Language and effect worksheet

Evaluation
Draw attention to the writing tip and ensure students understand the term 'evaluate' fully, before they write their response to Activity 4. Encourage peer assessment of the draft responses, which point out both strengths and areas for improvement.

Resources
Student Book 1: Activity 4, page 71

Lesson focus

Preparation and resources

- Student Book 1, pages 72–75
- Kerboodle worksheets:
  - 2.7 Language of the senses

What this lesson teaches and how

This lesson focuses on two non-fiction texts about the First World War in which the writers convey their feelings about their experiences. Extracts from Sassoon's 'Declaration' and Graves' *Good-Bye to All That* give students the opportunity to analyse the writers' use of language and to hone their comparative skills.

Skills and objectives

The following skills and Assessment Objectives (AOs) are addressed in this lesson:

- To analyse how writers use language to achieve effects and influence readers (AO2)
- To compare how writers convey ideas through language and tone (AO3)

Specification link

Paper 2, Section A, Questions 3 and 4

7 Fighting talk

Aberystwyth

Before students read the source text, play them a clip of a Welsh male voice choir singing 'Aberystwyth', a song that is mentioned in the text. Students may also be familiar with the Welsh tune 'Cwm Rhondda' from rugby matches. Briefly discuss the tradition of Welsh male choirs.

Onomatopoeia

If students need to refresh their understanding of onomatopoeia (in preparation for Activity 1), give them a few examples, e.g. crash, clatter. Then ask them to work in pairs, and to think of as many other examples of onomatopoeia as they can. Share with the whole class. If students struggle to think of examples, project images onto the whiteboard (e.g. a bee for 'buzz', a drum for 'bang', shattered glass for 'splinter', etc.).

Resources

Student Book 1: Activity 1, page 73

Support

Language of the senses

To support students with Activity 1b, distribute the worksheet 'Language of the senses' on Kerboodle. Ask them to fill in the columns according to whether they describe what the writer sees or hears. Discuss in pairs whether any of the words could fit into both columns.

Resources

Student Book 1: Activity 1b, page 73
Kerboodle: 2.7 Language of the senses worksheet

Support

Shell casings

Before students attempt Activity 2, show some images of WW1 shell casings, as some will find it difficult to evaluate the effectiveness of the words 'flop! flop!' without a visual image to help them. Students may also be interested to know that many WW1 survivors kept shell casings as souvenirs from the war, and some even turned them into works of art.

Student responses

When students are working on Activity 2, ensure that they understand just how weak Student B's response really is. No marks will be given by an examiner for generic comments such as 'The language makes the reader feel as if they were really there. It makes the description come alive.' Some GCSE English teachers actually ban these generic phrases!

Resources

Student Book 1: Activity 2, page 73

Wider reading

If students find the source text from Sassoon's 'A Soldier's Declaration' interesting, direct them towards Pat Barker's 'Regeneration' trilogy for more information about the complex circumstances surrounding this text. When discussing Sassoon's tone, they may also find it useful to read some of the poems in which he reflects on the war, such as 'The General' and 'Aftermath'.

Resources

Student Book 1: Activity 5, page 75
Weblink: http://siegfried-sassoon.
firstworldwarrelics.co.uk/html/
popular_poems.html

Stretch

Lesson focus

8 Operation Dynamo

Preparation and resources
- Student Book 1, pages 76–79
- Kerboodle worksheets:
  - 2.8 The language of film
  - 2.8 Storyboard support
  - 2.8 Progress check
  - 2.8 A defining moment in history

What this lesson teaches and how

This lesson enables students to pay close attention to the structure of a text, and the ways in which the writer presents information to the reader. Although the skills focus is on structural devices, this lesson lends itself to a variety of approaches, including the use of storyboarding and presentations.

Skills and objectives

The following skills and Assessment Objectives (AOs) are addressed in this lesson:
- To analyse how writers use structure to achieve effects (AO2)
- To evaluate texts critically and use appropriate evidence from texts (AO4)

Specification links

Paper 1, Section A, Question 4*
Paper 2, Section A, Question 3

*Note that AO4 is only tested in Paper 1, when students respond to fiction texts, but the skills are transferable between fiction and non-fiction texts.

Dunkirk evacuation footage

Before starting this lesson, check how much students already know about the evacuation of Dunkirk. If they are not familiar with this event, show some of the original film clips from the Internet (search for 'British Dunkirk evacuation'). As this footage is in black and white, it makes an interesting comparison with the source text, which emphasizes the colours of the flames in the night sky.

The language of film

Before students attempt Activity 1, revise the requirements of film storyboards. Use the worksheet 'The language of film' on Kerboodle to remind students of different camera angles and perspectives. You could also show a film trailer from a dramatic thriller such as *The Sixth Sense*, as this contains a range of camera shots and angles.

Resources
Student Book 1: Activity 1, page 77
Kerboodle: 2.8 The language of film worksheet

Storyboard support

For students who would find it difficult to complete a full storyboard, ask them to select three key moments from the text and to sketch the outline of the shot details, and choose which type of camera shot would work best. For extra support, distribute the worksheet 'Storyboard support' on Kerboodle to assist with this.

Resources
Student Book 1: Activity 1, page 77
Kerboodle: 2.8 Storyboard support worksheet

Support

Progress check

Give students copies of the Progress check worksheet on Kerboodle and ask them to evaluate the progress of their skills after studying the texts in the chapter and completing the activities.

Resources
Student Book 1: Progress check, page 79
Kerboodle: 2.8 Progress check worksheet

Presentation

Ask each student to prepare a short presentation entitled: 'A Defining Moment in History'. Their aim should be to inform and entertain the other students in their group. Students can focus on any event, which they have researched from anywhere in the world, including the evacuation of Dunkirk. After the presentations, ask students to evaluate two presentations of their choice, using the worksheet 'A defining moment in history' on Kerboodle.

Resources
Kerboodle: 2.8 A defining moment in history worksheet

Spoken Language opportunity

Unit 4: Assessment

Assessment Objectives

All six reading and writing Assessment Objectives (AOs) are addressed in this unit (AO1, AO2, AO3, AO4, AO5, AO6).

Why do we have an assessment unit?

The final unit in each chapter of *AQA GCSE English Language Student Book 1* focuses on assessment. These units give students an opportunity to practise the skills they have developed throughout the chapter. Regular formal assessments will help to monitor students' progress and assist with target-setting. Some teachers may wish to break down the assessment unit into individual activities or chunks; others may prefer to use the assessment in its entirety, to be completed under exam-type conditions, where the questions are given a set timing.

Many of the activities in this unit build up to assessment questions which echo the tasks that will be set in exam Paper 1 or Paper 2, providing early practice for responding to exam-style questions. A summary of the relationship between the assessment units and exam paper questions can be found on pages 102–103 of this Teacher Companion.

Working through Chapter 2 'Fight for freedom', students will be developing some of the essential reading and writing skills for their GCSE exam. This unit will assess whether they have grasped these skills and if they can demonstrate how to employ them in an assessment situation.

What are students demonstrating?

Reading

Students will be able to:

- identify information within a text
- summarize and compare writers' ideas
- analyse how a writer uses language and structure for effect
- evaluate what a writer does to make their writing successful.

Writing

Students will be able to:

- plan, write and proofread a first-person account.

How to deliver the assessment

You might wish to separate the reading and writing assessment activities into two separate lessons. Look at the questions in all of the activities and, if students are completing these under exam-type conditions, emphasize the importance of time management. A Word document version of the end of chapter assessment is available on Kerboodle which can be assigned to students.

Understanding the assessment

If necessary, allow time to discuss what is expected in the assessment activities.

Remind students to look carefully at the wording of the questions:

- If they are told to refer to a specific part of the source text, they must ensure that they do focus on that part, and not get distracted by the rest of the text.

- They should note key words used in the questions, such as 'summarize', 'compare', 'explain', 'language', 'structure' and 'character'. Emphasize that these words give a clear indication of what students should be focusing on, and how they should present their response.

- Warn students to check whether the question refers to just one source text or two.

- If the question contains bullet points, students should check that they do cover each point in their response and not just focus on the first one.

Support

Offer support when requested. The aim of the assessment activities is to familiarize students with working in exam-type conditions with time constraints and precise instructions. It is also to build each student's confidence in preparation for the real exam and to coach students on exam techniques as appropriate.

Marking

Activity 1 and Activity 5 can be marked using the suggested answers overleaf. This can be done either by teachers or as peer/self-assessment. The longer, more evaluative tasks, for example the 'how' questions, can be marked using the 'Skills descriptors' in the relevant Paper 1 or Paper 2 AQA Specimen mark scheme on pages 107–112 of this Teacher Companion. Sample responses (at Level 2 and Level 4) with examiner comments for Activity 2d are available on Kerboodle.

Use the chart on page 102 of this Teacher Companion to identify which question in the end-of-chapter assessment relates to which exam paper question. If the assessment responses are produced under exam conditions, bear this in mind when marking the assessments. When marking the evaluative responses, you will want to mark using the 'best fit' principle, which means that not all points in the 'Skills descriptors' need to be demonstrated in order to achieve a mark in that level. Nor will those skills necessarily be used consistently throughout the response. Finally, you will need to make a judgement, based on your professional experience and using the AQA sample student responses (available on the AQA website, www.aqa.org.uk), on points such as 'range', 'relevance' and 'accuracy' as used within the 'Skills descriptors' in the mark scheme.

AQA GCSE English Language Student Book 1 answers

Below are the answers to any largely non-subjective *Student Book 1* activities contained within this chapter.

Lesson 1 Written in black and white

Activity 1

'cannot gain lodging in the motels of the highways and the hotels of the cities'

'our children are stripped of their selfhood'; 'For Whites Only'

'a Negro in Mississippi cannot vote'

Lesson 2 Sugar and spice

Activity 2

a. He realized that violent intimidation wasn't working and decided to try other tactics including pleading and bribery.

b. The manager was suggesting that women acting on stage was unnatural and, although women could technically be trained to act, they would be objects of ridicule.

c. Judith was looking for someone who would take her seriously, and offer her advice or employment. She knew of no other way to make contact with actors or managers.

Activity 6

a. Patronizing (radio script); frustrated (newspaper article)

b. 'I'm not suggesting that we're reaching the stage when husbands stay at home and run the house while the wives go out and earn the money – No!' (patronizing)
'there was no obvious disintegration of society as a result' (frustration)

Lesson 3 Speaking out

Activity 1

a. Students' responses might include some of the following: Stonewall has commissioned research into homophobic abuse at football games; the research was conducted by YouGov; over 2,000 fans from across Britain were surveyed; football 'insiders', including lesbian and gay players, were also interviewed; according to the survey, 7 out of 10 fans have witnessed homophobic abuse at football games; the research suggests that most fans want to see sanctions against this abuse; 3 out of 5 fans believe that homophobic abuse deters players from coming out; 2 out of 3 fans would feel comfortable if a player on their team came out; over half of the fans surveyed would like to see more sanctions from the FA in response to anti-gay abuse at football games; the FA is calling for immediate action against homophobic abuse.

b. The writer feels that anti-gay abuse at football matches is cause for immediate concern, and would support sanctions from the FA. This issue needs to be addressed urgently if England is to host major international tournaments.

c. The tone is assertive and uncompromising in an attempt to convince the reader of the scale of the problem and the urgent need for solutions.

Lesson 7 Fighting talk

Activity 1

a. Alliteration: flat on our faces

Onomatopoeia: buzzing, whizzed, CRASH, hissing, burst, flop! flop!

Noun phrases: broken trees, dull red clay, jagged little piece, red flash, flare-lights, hollow bang, unlit suburb

Verbs: dazzled

Repetition: louder and louder

Assessment unit

Activity 1

a. The school building was Victorian; there was a large grey playground; it was surrounded by a high wire fence; there was hopscotch on the ground; there was a bull's eye on one wall.

Activity 5

a. On his arrival, Heathcliff was dirty, black-haired and dressed in rags; his face looked older than Catherine's; his speech was unclear; he had no family; he had no home; he was living in the streets of Liverpool; he was starving.

Chapter overview

Why are we teaching this?

This chapter is designed to develop students' skills in reading, writing and spoken English by exposing them to a range of texts on the theme of being trapped. The source texts focus on both real people and fictional characters who have found themselves physically, mentally or emotionally ensnared in situations beyond their control.

As students work though this chapter, they will have the opportunity to develop their reading skills, focusing closely on language and structure choices that the writers have made, and the effects that they have created for the reader. In addition, students will have the opportunity to write imaginatively and to present a personal viewpoint about a particular topic.

A range of speaking and listening tasks have been embedded into the lessons, and students are encouraged to develop their learning through discussion and collaboration with others.

What are the learning aims?

The main skills and learning objectives have been summarized at the start of each lesson in *AQA GCSE English language Student Book 1*. They are all linked to aspects of the Assessment Objectives (AOs), which are also flagged at the start of each lesson.

By the end of this chapter, students will be developing all of the major skills required by the AQA English Language course. They will be able to:

- read texts closely in order to identify and interpret information and ideas (AO1)
- select and summarize evidence from texts to support a viewpoint (AO1)
- examine how the writer's word choice influences the reader (AO2)
- analyse how the writer uses discourse markers to guide the reader (AO2)
- compare writers' ideas and perspectives (AO3)
- evaluate how effectively writers create atmosphere and tension (AO4)
- evaluate how effectively the writer uses contrast (AO4)
- communicate clearly and imaginatively in their own writing (AO5)
- experiment with a range of sentence structures and vocabulary for effect (AO6)
- organize ideas so that writing is clear and accurate (AO6).

How will this be assessed?

Activities within each lesson

Teachers can choose to assess some or all of the activities within each lesson. Some activities have been designed to encourage students to work collaboratively; others are designed to encourage students to develop their independent learning skills and build their reading stamina.

Progress check

The second unit ends with a Progress check (on page 111), which encourages students to reflect on areas of strength and weakness in their learning. This could be completed in collaboration with the teacher or teaching assistant, or with peers, so that students gain a realistic impression of their relative strengths and areas for development.
A Progress check is also available on Kerboodle and can be adapted to reflect the breadth of attainment within the class. Ideally, the Progress checks will enable teachers to adapt their teaching in subsequent chapters if areas of weakness have been identified, when the same skills are revisited and developed.

Assessment unit

The assessment unit focuses on the reading and writing skills covered in this chapter, and gives students the opportunity to revise and practise them in a series of activities, using source texts similar to the ones that they will encounter in their exams.

Spoken Language

Teachers will need to offer opportunities for the assessment of Spoken English throughout the course. See pages 122–123 of this Teacher Companion for more information. Activities that could be developed into Spoken Language tasks have been flagged in each lesson.

Lesson sequence

Below is a suggested lesson sequence, but you might choose to alter or add to it to suit your particular teaching needs. Note that the material involved in some of the lessons outlined may be covered over two or more teaching sessions.

Introducing the chapter

- Introduce the main subject of the chapter: trapped.
- Discuss students' reactions to the topic and establish whether they have any personal experience of the issues covered in the chapter.
- Outline the reading and writing skills that will be covered within the AOs.
- Explain that this chapter will enable students to practise their skills for all AOs.

1 Survival of the fittest	2 Turtle trap	3 Let's talk about it
• Explore the origin of the lesson title. • Respond to the articles about Aron Ralston and Annie McNeal. • Summarize evidence from the texts and compare the writers' perspectives.	• Explore an extract from Liz Cleere's travel blog. • Analyse the ways in which the author has used language to create powerful effects for the reader.	• Prepare for writing by exploring the use of dialogue in a short story. • Plan and write a continuation of the dialogue. • Focus on the use of direct speech and speech punctuation.
4 Fighting back	**5 A giant in science**	**6 The shackles of poverty**
• Respond to the opening of a short story and an extract from an autobiographical account. • Examine how the writer uses language and structure to create tension. • Compare the writers' ideas and perspectives.	• Respond to a newspaper article about Professor Stephen Hawking. • Examine how the writer uses language and discourse markers to influence and guide the reader.	• Prepare for discursive writing by researching a controversial topic. • Plan and write an article that clearly communicates a point of view.
7 Time warp	**8 For better or worse?**	**Assessment**
• Respond to the extract from *Great Expectations* in which Dickens introduces Miss Havisham. • Explore the use of contrast and imagery. • Use evidence from the text to evaluate the writer's use of language.	• Respond to a recent newspaper article and a fiction text about forced marriage. • Identify and interpret ideas. • Compare writers' ideas and perspectives.	• Use the Progress chart on page 111 of the Student Book to assess the level of skill achieved in order to plan further action and to prioritize revision and practice. • Unit 3 revises the skills required by the reading and writing Assessment Objectives covered in the chapter and offers opportunity for further practice.

Preparing to teach

Refresh your knowledge

You might find it helpful to consider the following key points when planning your teaching of this chapter:

- Some students may already be familiar with true stories that contain accounts of resilience, determination and endurance. Harrowing autobiographical accounts based on hardship in early life may help to draw some reluctant readers into the world of literary non-fiction. Keying 'biographies for teenagers' into a search engine should produce a list of the most contemporary popular texts. Classic stories of endurance and resilience by writers such as Anne Frank, Frank McCourt, Maya Angelou, Joe Simpson, Adeline Yen Mah and Dave Pelzer have stood the test of time and remain popular with more confident teenage readers.

- The theme of being trapped – either physically or emotionally – is also popular in fiction, and can be found in almost every genre. For example, some students may have already encountered series at KS3 that contain teenage protagonists battling against the forces of evil. Even the more reluctant readers may be aware of the 'Young Bond' series by Charlie Higson, the 'Cherub' series by Robert Muchamore, the 'Adventure' series by Anthony McGowan based on the novels of Willard Price and the 'Hunger Games' trilogy by Suzanne Collins.

Links and further reading

- The full text of Alan Paton's classic story 'The Waste Land' can be found online. Students may be interested to learn more about this pioneering man who worked as the principal of a reform school in South Africa, and introduced progressive reforms to support the teenagers in his care. Despite achieving critical success as a writer, with novels such as *Cry, the Beloved Country*, Paton continued to be an anti-apartheid campaigner and activist all his life. See: http://www.sahistory.org.za/people/alan-stewart-paton

- An extract from Samantha Barlow's autobiographical account *Left for Dead* is currently available on Penguin's Australian website: http://www.penguin.com.au/products/9781921901799/left-dead-true-story-resilience-and-courage/358655/extract

- Students with an interest in Professor Stephen Hawking's work, but little theoretical background, might find *George's Secret Key to the Universe* interesting. Hawking published the book in 2007 with his daughter, Lucy; its stated purpose was 'to explain theoretical physics in an accessible way to youngsters'. More ambitious young scientists might like to try Hawking's *A Brief History of Time*, which stayed on the British *Sunday Times* bestsellers list for a record-breaking 237 weeks.

- Although 19th-century fiction will not appear in the English Language GCSE exam papers, it does feature in the Literature course, and students can only gain by further exposure to the work of Charles Dickens. Encourage students to familiarize themselves with more of his novels – offering key extracts for low-attaining students who might struggle to read the complete novels independently. Draw attention to his skills with characterization, plot development, use of language and his exposure of social problems in Victorian England.

- Encourage students to read works by Hanif Kureishi, and to explore some of the controversial issues that he tackles. For example, *My Son The Fanatic* (religious extremism), *My Beautiful Laundrette* (racism and homophobia).

- If students aren't already familiar with it, introduce them to *The Diary of a Young Girl: Anne Frank*. Explain the context of her 'entrapment' during the Nazi occupation of the Netherlands.

- Travel writers with a story to tell can provide powerful inspiration for students' own writing. Bill Bryson is usually popular; other writers to recommend include Jan Morris, Bruce Chatwin, Sarah Wheeler and Robert MacFarlane and Paul Theroux.

Please note that OUP is not responsible for the third-party content. Although all links were correct at the time of publication, the content and location of this material may change.

| **Planning guidelines and teaching tips** | Think about how you can make the materials relevant to your students and responsive to their particular needs and learning targets. Some suggested approaches to address key areas are provided below. |

- Wherever possible, provide opportunities for students to **discuss and debate** the issues that are raised in the texts they study.

- **Modelling responses** to reading would be beneficial for many students in this chapter. If possible, co-construct answers on the whiteboard. Gradually remove the scaffolding as students become more confident about constructing their own responses. Teach the phrase 'This phrase suggests…' to encourage a focused response to short quotations.

- When they are preparing for their own writing, encourage students to take on board **factual information** which may challenge the viewpoints they have assimilated. For example, the 2014 report from the Joseph Rowntree Foundation on 'Monitoring Poverty and Social Exclusion' reveals dramatic changes in those most at risk of poverty compared to ten years ago.

- Encourage students to **read newspaper articles** on topics of interest to them. Online news sites are readily accessible to most students. On his 'Pick 'n' Mix Blog', Geoff Barton provides examples of well-written articles, which students may find interesting.

- As students gain confidence in communicating their own opinions in writing, encourage them to seek out real-life audiences by using **local and national journalism competitions**. Also suggest that students use their school community as an audience, e.g. through writing submissions for the school's website.

- Refer to the **Grammar Reference Guide** on Kerboodle for definitions and examples of specific grammatical features covered by this chapter.

- Plan carefully for differentiation, using the **Support and Stretch activities** in the Student Book, and the additional ideas offered in the individual lesson support sections in this Teacher Companion.

Lesson focus

Preparation and resources
- Student Book 1, pages 86–89
- Kerboodle worksheets:
  - 3.1 Understanding information
  - 3.1 Summarizing information
  - 3.1 Comparing and contrasting

What this lesson teaches and how

This lesson focuses on the real experiences of two individuals who survived terrible accidents. It enables students to identify and interpret textual evidence from two different centuries and contexts, and summarize the links between the two.

Skills and objectives

The following skills and Assessment Objectives (AOs) are addressed in this lesson:
- To identify and interpret ideas and information (AO1)
- To select and synthesize evidence from different texts (AO1)

Specification link

Paper 2, Section A, Questions 1 and 2

1 Survival of the fittest

Endurance

Discuss any real-life stories in which an individual survived through determination and endurance. Students may volunteer stories based on their own experience. Others may know of Joe Simpson: there are several clips on the Internet in which Joe speaks of his extraordinary experience, described in *Touching the Void*.

Resources

Find video clips of Joe Simpson on the Internet

Geographical context

Before reading the source text about Aron Ralston, show students an image or some film footage of the Utah Canyonlands at sunset. The visual images should support students' comprehension of explicit information within the text.

Resources

Weblinks: http://www.shutterstock.com/video/clip-7198927-stock-footage-beautiful-sunset-near-the-marlboro-point-canyonlands-utah.html
http://www.shutterstock.com/pic-151853069.html

True or false?

To support Activity 1, distribute the worksheet 'Understanding information' on Kerboodle. Note that there are some additional questions to those in the Student Book.

Resources

Student Book 1: Activity 1, page 87
Kerboodle: 3.1 Understanding information worksheet

SPAG

19th-century context

Ensure that all students are familiar with the context of Annie McNeal's accident. They may have seen historical documentaries or TV dramas set at the time of the Industrial Revolution. If not, show them some images of 19th-century mill machinery and emphasize that these machines were often driven by children under the age of 16.

Summarizing information

To support Activities 4 and 5, distribute the worksheet 'Summarizing information' on Kerboodle. Encourage students to summarize the information using some short quotations and their own words.

Resources

Student Book 1: Activities 4 and 5, page 89
Kerboodle: 3.1 Summarizing information worksheet

Support

Comparing and contrasting

Before students attempt Activity 5, it may be useful to model some different ways in which students can compare and contrast information on the board. For additional practice, distribute the worksheet 'Comparing and contrasting' on Kerboodle and spend some time revising conjunctions and adverbials.

Resources

Student Book 1: Activity 5, page 89
Kerboodle: 3.1 Comparing and contrasting worksheet

SPAG

Lesson focus

Preparation and resources
- Student Book 1, pages 90–91
- Kerboodle worksheets:
  - 3.2 Word choices
  - 3.2 Synonyms

What this lesson teaches and how

In this lesson, students will analyse a travel writing blog that was entered for a national competition. They will have the opportunity to focus closely on the writer's choice of words and imagery and explore the effects of these choices. Alternative vocabulary will also be considered and assessed for its impact on the reader.

Skills and objectives

The following skills and Assessment Objectives (AOs) are addressed in this lesson:
- To examine how the writer's word choice influences the reader (AO2)
- To select evidence from the text to support views (AO2)

Specification link

Paper 2, Section A, Question 3

2 Turtle trap

Metaphors

Before students start work on Activity 1, revise extended metaphors with them. Refer to the poem 'Nettles', by Vernon Scannell, which contains an extended military metaphor. This reference to poetry is a useful crossover with skills linked to the AQA Literature GCSE, if students are also preparing for that.

Resources

Student Book 1: Activity 1, page 90
Weblink: http://www.poemhunter.com/poem/nettles/

Stretch

Where in the world?

Explain that the blog by Liz Cleere was the runner-up for a *Guardian* travel writing award. Ask students where in the world they would like to visit, and to explain their reasons to the rest of the class in a formal presentation. This could be done as an individual, paired or group activity.

Spoken Language opportunity

Word choice

When considering their word choices for Activity 2, distribute the worksheet 'Word choices' on Kerboodle. Encourage students to focus on both sound and meaning. Emphasize the plosive and alliterative sounds of Cleere's choices.

Resources

Student Book 1: Activity 2, page 91
Kerboodle: 3.2 Word choices worksheet

Support

Synonyms

To support some students in responding to Activity 3, give them the worksheet 'Synonyms' on Kerboodle. This shows them some (bland) synonyms for the highlighted words in the extract, and should help them to evaluate the effectiveness of the word chosen by Liz Cleere.

Resources

Student Book 1: Activity 3, page 91
Kerboodle: 3.2 Synonyms worksheet

Support

Peer assessment

Encourage students to peer-assess each other's work once first drafts have been completed. Suggest specific criteria for the assessment, e.g. inclusion of quotations, specific description of effects, clear, accurate spelling and punctuation. Encourage students to feed back to each other, with positive and constructive comments and suggestions.

Resources

Student Book 1: Activity 4, page 91

Lesson focus

Preparation and resources

- Student Book 1, pages 92–93
- Kerboodle worksheets:
  - 3.3 Stage directions
  - 3.3 What happens next

What this lesson teaches and how

In this lesson, students will read an extract from a novel and have the opportunity to make predictions about the text. The lesson provides an opportunity to analyse how writers present dialogue in a text, using correct punctuation and presentation. Students will also write a continuation of the dialogue, practising the skills they have just analysed.

Skills and objectives

The following skills and Assessment Objectives (AOs) are addressed in this lesson:

- To communicate imaginatively, in particular through dialogue (AO5)
- To organize ideas so that writing is clear and accurate (AO6)

Specification link

Paper 1, Section B, Question 5

3 Let's talk about it

Sharing novels

In preparation for the lesson, ask students to bring in a novel they have read that contains character-revealing dialogue. Students share their ideas with a small group. Encourage them to notice the ways in which some authors use non-standard forms of English to convey information about character and add a sense of realism. Alternatively, use a section of dialogue from a novel read at KS3, or one of the GCSE English Literature set novels.

Predictions

Before students read the source text, ask them whether they have read any books and/or seen any films from the 'kidnapping' genre. Their responses to Activity 1a are likely to draw on their previous experience of the genre. As the possible kidnapping of a woman by a man is a sensitive topic, ask students to produce a response that challenges stereotypical ideas or includes a twist or humorous development instead.

Resources

Student Book 1: Activity 1, page 92
Weblinks: https://www.goodreads.com/shelf/show/kidnapping
http://www.screenjunkies.com/movies/genres-movies/drama/10-best-kidnapped-movies/

Planning dialogue

Some students might find it helpful to sketch out a simple cartoon strip with speech bubbles to show what happens next in their story. The worksheet 'What happens next' on Kerboodle could be used to support this. Remind students that speech bubbles contain direct speech but do not need quotation marks. However, when they convert their images to narrative text, they do need to use full punctuation.

Resources

Student Book 1: Activity 2a, page 93
Kerboodle: 3.3 What happens next worksheet

Self- and peer-assessment

After proofreading their own work, ask students to swap their work with a partner and check it against the six rules of punctuation listed in the Student Book (page 93).

Resources

Student Book 1: Activity 2, page 93

Positive feedback

Ask students to nominate narratives to be read aloud. If the nominated writers are willing to participate in the process, ask the group to vote anonymously for the narrative they feel has the most interesting and original conclusion, with one or two sentences explaining their choice. Pass any positive feedback back to the authors!

Dialogue stage directions

Distribute the worksheet 'Stage directions' on Kerboodle. Remind students that stage directions can tell actors how they should speak, as well as how they should move. Ask students to work in pairs and to decide how each part of the dialogue might be spoken. They will need to infer the tone of each utterance. On completion, invite a few pairs to read out their versions, following their own stage directions.

Resources

Kerboodle: 3.3 Stage directions worksheet

Lesson focus

Preparation and resources
- Student Book 1, pages 94–99
- Kerboodle worksheets:
  - 3.4 Danger!
  - 3.4 Sea of perils
  - 3.4 Past or present

What this lesson teaches and how

This lesson introduces students to two extracts that describe an attack on an individual in a dark street. They will evaluate the ways in which the writers create tension through the use of language, setting and structure. They will then have the opportunity to compare the writers' ideas and perspectives.

Skills and objectives

The following skills and Assessment Objectives (AOs) are addressed in this lesson:
- To evaluate how effectively the writer creates tension (AO4)
- To compare writers' ideas and perspectives (AO3)

Specification links

Paper 1, Section A, Question 4*
Paper 2, Section A, Question 4*

*Note that although AO3 (comparison) is only tested in Paper 2 with non-fiction texts, and AO4 (evaluation) is only tested in Paper 1 with a fiction text, both skills are relevant to fiction and non-fiction texts.

4 Fighting back

Junkyard setting

Before reading the source text for the first time, show students the opening of the 'Chopper in the Junkyard' clip from the film *Stand By Me*. Ask students to note down anything they spotted in the background which helps to create the setting, e.g. piles of old tyres. Another option is the fight scene in the scrapyard from the film *Stormbreaker*. This focus on detail prepares students for the written extracts.

Danger!

To support Activity 2, distribute the worksheet 'Danger!' on Kerboodle. Before students discuss their notes with a partner, feed in any words and concepts that might be useful, e.g. urge of adrenaline, fight or flight, pre-emptive strike. Take a poll asking the class whether they think the man's actions were brave or reckless.

Resources

Student Book 1: Activity 2, page 96
Kerboodle: 3.4 Danger! worksheet

Analysing the simile

Distribute the worksheet 'Sea of perils' on Kerboodle. Ask students to note down any 'perils' they can think of which threaten the safety and well-being of the man trapped on the island. They should also note how those perils might make the man feel. Move students beyond sharks to other forms of threat to his well-being!

Resources

Student Book 1: Activity 3, page 97
Kerboodle: 3.4 Sea of perils worksheet

Support

Past or present

Before students work on Activity 6, ask them to write out the source text in the past tense, then decide which version creates more tension. Ensure students can identify the verbs, especially those which appear in contracted forms. The worksheet 'Past or present' on Kerboodle supports this activity.

Resources

Student Book 1: Activity 6, page 99
Kerboodle: 3.4 Past or present worksheet

SPAG and Support

Setting

When responding to Activity 7, students may highlight the fact that there is not much description of setting in the Australian account. Ask students, working in pairs, to write three sentences to add to the first paragraph to evoke the setting of the deserted streets and build up the tension.

Resources

Student Book 1: Activity 7, page 99

Further reading

Encourage students to read the full short story 'The Waste Land' by Alan Paton, and also more of the extract from *Left for Dead: a True Story of Resilience and Courage* by Samantha and Laurence Barlow.

Stretch

Lesson focus

Preparation and resources

- Student Book 1, pages 100–101
- Kerboodle worksheets:
  - 3.5 Revising conjunctions

What this lesson teaches and how

This lesson is based on an article about the renowned scientist Professor Stephen Hawking. Although the focus is on the structural devices used to influence the reader, students will also have the opportunity to focus on the impact of other aspects of the journalist's language.

Skills and objectives

The following skills and Assessment Objectives (AOs) are addressed in this lesson:

- To examine how the writer uses key sentences, phrases and discourse markers to influence the reader (AO2)
- To select evidence from the text to support views (AO2)

Specification link

Paper 2, Section A, Question 3

5 A giant in science

MND Association

Before starting this lesson, provide students with some background information about Motor Neurone Disease. The MND Association website contains a lot of useful information. Relate this condition to the theme of 'trapped' and discuss how technology can be liberating.

Resources

Weblink:
http://www.mndassociation.org/

Revising conjunctions

Revise the role of conjunctions to link clauses in a sentence. Some conjunctions can also be described as 'discourse markers' (but not all). Give out the worksheet 'Revising conjunctions' from Kerboodle and encourage students to complete the activities. This should reinforce their grammatical awareness and help with their own writing. A more detailed explanation of conjunctions (coordinating and subordinating) can be found in the Grammar Reference Guide.

Resources

Kerboodle: 3.5 Revising conjunctions worksheet

SPAG and Support

Withholding information

Before they start making notes for Activity 2, ask students to decide which they consider to be the three most important pieces of factual information that are included in this article, and to note whereabouts in the article these pieces of information are included. Draw their attention to the fact that key information is often withheld by writers until the final paragraphs.

Final paragraph

Before writing their response to Activity 2, ask students to focus closely on the final paragraph. Ask them to discuss in pairs three choices that the writer made in that paragraph to convey their message that Stephen Hawking is a hero. Draw out the use of two powerful adjectives with strong plosive sounds: 'unique' and 'great'; the impact of the single-word sentence: 'Uplifted'; the use of alliteration in the words 'happy' and 'hero'.

Overcoming the odds

Stephen Hawking features in a list compiled by Biography Online entitled 'People who overcame difficult odds'. This list contains some of the most inspiring people in recent history. Place students in small groups, and ask them to choose three individuals whom they would like to invite to the school to give motivational talks. At least one name should come from the list. Each group should present their ideas formally to the class.

Resources

Weblink:
http://www.biographyonline.net/people/overcame-difficult-odds.html

Spoken Language opportunity

A true hero or heroine

Challenge higher attaining students to research a hero or heroine of their choice, who they believe overcame difficult odds, then to write an article about them for a magazine. Encourage them to think carefully about word choice and structure in order to convince the reader that their chosen person is worthy of the title 'hero' or 'heroine'.

Stretch

Lesson focus

6 The shackles of poverty

Preparation and resources
- Student Book 1, pages 102–105
- Kerboodle worksheets:
  - 3.6 On the streets
  - 3.6 What is society?

What this lesson teaches and how

Having analysed a variety of texts and undertaken some written tasks, students will be starting to develop their skills as authors. This lesson will enable them to practise the elements of discursive writing, using a controversial statement as the stimulus.

Skills and objectives

The following skills and Assessment Objectives (AOs) are addressed in this lesson:
- To communicate discursively, in particular by presenting a point of view (AO5)
- To organize ideas so that writing is clear and accurate (AO6)

Specification link

Paper 2, Section B, Question 5

Background information

Ensure students have some understanding of the range of reasons that might lead to people begging for money in the UK. Introduce them to different viewpoints. Encourage some research and discussion prior to the lesson.

Resources

Stone Cold by Robert Swindells
Weblinks: http://www.shelterclassroomkit.org.uk/
http://www.theguardian.com/commentisfree/2013/dec/06/dont-give-money-beggars-help-them

Controversial statement

The statement in the Student Book is designed to be controversial, but be aware that this topic may be painful for students whose families have experienced problems with housing. Use the 'On the streets' worksheet on Kerboodle to generate discussion. Ask students which of the people they would be most willing to give money to, and why.

Resources

Kerboodle: 3.6 On the streets worksheet

What is society?

Before students write their plan for Activity 1, distribute the worksheet 'What is society' on Kerboodle. Ask students to complete the mind map. Who is included? Who is not? Draw attention to the pronouns 'they' and 'us' in the controversial statement and explain that these are not 'fixed' concepts. Different students in the group may have different relationships with these words, and with the word 'society'.

Resources

Student Book 1: Activity 1, page 103
Kerboodle: 3.6 What is society? worksheet

Definition of society

Challenge higher attaining students to come up with a definition of the word 'society', after completing the mind map. The *Oxford Student's Dictionary* defines it as 'an organized community of people in a particular country or region'.

Stretch

Effective vocabulary

To support Activity 4, give students the text of another article on the subject of begging which contains effective vocabulary choices and emotive language features. Ask them to highlight as many examples as they can find. Draw their attention to both the meaning and sound of words, the tone, imagery and variation of sentence structures. Jeremy Swain's blog would work well in this context.

Resources

Student Book 1: Activity 4, page 105
Weblink: http://jeremyswain.blogspot.co.uk/2013/10/killing-with-kindness.html

Presenting a viewpoint

Remind students to proofread their work. If you feel they need to revise any specific grammatical structures, refer to the Grammar Reference Guide and SPAG interactives on Kerboodle.

Students could develop their writing into a formal presentation as a Spoken Language task. Ensure students are given sufficient time to add visuals to their presentation, to rehearse, and that they are aware of how their GCSE Spoken Language task will be assessed.

SPAG and Spoken Language opportunity

Lesson focus

Preparation and resources
- Student Book 1, pages 106–107
- Kerboodle worksheets:
  - 3.7 First impressions
  - 3.7 Positive and negative

What this lesson teaches and how

This lesson allows students to explore characterization through their reading of an extract from Charles Dickens's novel *Great Expectations*. In the extract, the narrator describes his first meeting with Miss Havisham. Students will evaluate the ways in which Dickens uses contrast to depict this character.

Skills and objectives

The following skills and Assessment Objectives (AOs) are addressed in this lesson:
- To evaluate how effectively the writer uses contrast (AO4)
- To select evidence from the text to support views (AO4)

Specification link

Paper 1, Section A, Question 4*

*Note that in Paper 1 of the exam, students will be responding to 20th- and 21st-century fiction extracts. However, looking at this 19th-century fiction extract is valid, because the skills used are transferable to both fiction and non-fiction texts from any century.

7 Time warp

Setting the context

Show students images of Victorian wedding dresses, in particular Queen Victoria's. Point out that white was often worn by wealthy women because before the days of easy bleaching, it was the most expensive 'colour' to produce. Lace was popular on wedding dresses, partly because Queen Victoria wanted to promote the lace-making cottage industries, which had been badly hit by urban industrialization.

Resources
Weblink: http://thedreamstress. com/2011/04/queen-victorias- wedding-dress-the-one-that-started- it-all/queen_victoria/

First impressions

To support Activity 1a, give students the worksheet 'First impressions' on Kerboodle. Encourage discussion about what these first impressions imply about Miss Havisham (she is wealthy, likes luxuries, she is preparing for a journey or an event, things have been interrupted and are now slightly chaotic).

Resources
Student Book 1: Activity 1a, page 107
Kerboodle: 3.7 First impressions worksheet

Support

Positive and negative

To ensure that students have understood the meaning and implications of the key vocabulary and contrasting images, distribute the worksheet 'Positive and negative' on Kerboodle. If necessary, revise the word 'connotations' first by giving students words such as: dentist, theme park, chocolate, olives, and discuss their associations.

Resources
Student Book 1: Activity 1, page 107
Kerboodle: 3.7 Positive and negative worksheet

Dickens as a social commentator

Encourage higher attaining students to familiarize themselves with more of Dickens' novels and to identify his concerns about society (e.g. the workhouse in *Oliver Twist*, brutal schools in *Nicholas Nickleby*, the effects of industrialization in *Hard Times*, the plight of the working poor in *A Christmas Carol*). This could be developed into a presentation about 'Dickens as a social commentator'.

Havisham

Display the poem 'Havisham' by Carol Ann Duffy. Ask students what they can infer about Miss Havisham's bitter experience and her state of mind. Challenge students to look at how the poet uses contrast in this poem to portray her character. Although there is no poetry in the AQA English Language GCSE, many students will also be studying the AQA Literature GCSE.

Resources
Weblink: http://www.scottishpoetrylibrary. org.uk/poetry/poems/havisham

Stretch

Favourite characters

Introduce, or remind students of other famous characters depicted by Dickens, e.g. The Artful Dodger in *Oliver Twist*, Uriah Heep in *David Copperfield*, Ebenezer Scrooge in *A Christmas Carol*. Ask them to find a description of them in the relevant novel and then write a few paragraphs about how effectively Dickens presents this character. They should think about word choice, connotations, imagery, use of contrast and any other literary devices used to create impact for the reader.

Lesson focus

Preparation and resources
- Student Book 1, pages 108–111
- Kerboodle worksheets:
  - 3.8 Making comparisons
  - 3.8 Progress check

What this lesson teaches and how

In this lesson, students will read two texts on the theme of forced marriages – one fiction, one non-fiction. They will have the opportunity to discuss and interpret the information in the texts and compare the very different treatments of the same topic.

Skills and objectives

The following skills and Assessment Objectives (AOs) are addressed in this lesson:
- To identify and interpret information and ideas (AO1)
- To compare writers' ideas and perspectives (AO3)

Specification links

Paper 1, Section A, Question 1
Paper 2, Section A, Question 1 and 4*

*Note that the students will be required to compare two non-fiction texts in Paper 2 (AO3), but the same skills are involved when using fiction and non-fiction texts.

8 For better or worse?

Good parenting

Before starting this lesson, ask students to work in groups and compile a list of ten qualities that good parents have. There are plenty of websites containing parenting advice, and you could ask each group to do some research and present their findings, and their opinions, to the class.

Resources

Weblinks: http://www.parenting. co.uk/help/talking-to-teenagers.cfm http://www.independent.co.uk/ voices/comment/what-makes-a- good-parent-its-not-discipline-or- striving-for-respect-or-fear-above-all- else-its-trust-8348741.html

Arranged marriage

Ask students to list possible advantages and disadvantages of arranged marriages. Ensure they understand the difference between an 'arranged' and a 'forced' marriage. Encourage students to read first-person accounts of people who have had successful arranged marriages, so they have sufficient information to weigh up the pros and cons.

Resources

Weblink:
http://www.theguardian.com/ lifeandstyle/2008/sep/13/family1

Making comparisons

Distribute the worksheet 'Making comparisons' on Kerboodle to support students with Activity 2. Although the two texts are linked by theme, they are very different in terms of genre, narrative voice, language and structure. Many students find it difficult to discuss tone, so pre-teaching relevant vocabulary may be helpful.

Resources

Student Book 1: Activity 2, page 110
Kerboodle: 3.8 Making comparisons worksheet

Support

Happy ending?

Ask students to work with a partner and write three predictions about how Sara's story develops. Point out that the blog appeared in *The Guardian* several years after the events described, and this should provide a clue. Then read the final part of the blog aloud to the class. Encourage students to discuss to what extent they feel this story had a 'happy' ending.

Resources

Weblink: http://freedomcharity.org. uk/blog/116/

Hanif Kureishi

Challenge students to find out more about the life and work of Hanif Kureishi. Encourage them to compile an overview of the themes that he tackles in his work, in his novels, plays and screenplays, and to explore how they link to his own life experiences. Alternatively, students could focus on another writer who draws on his or her experience of life in another country. The outcome could be a written summary, or developed into a presentation for Spoken Language.

Stretch and Spoken Language

Progress check

Give students copies of the Progress check worksheet on Kerboodle and ask them to evaluate the progress of their skills after studying the texts in the chapter and completing the activities.

Resources

Student Book 1: Progress check, page 111
Kerboodle: 3.8 Progress check worksheet

Unit 3: Assessment

Preparation and resources

- Student Book 1 pages 112–115
- Teacher Companion – pages 107–112 [mark schemes] and 103 [chart showing links between assessment questions and exam paper questions]
- Kerboodle:
  - 3 Assessment
  - 3 Sample responses with examiner's comments

Assessment Objectives

All six reading and writing Assessment Objectives (AOs) are addressed in this unit (AO1, AO2, AO3, AO4, AO5, AO6).

Why do we have an assessment unit?

The final unit in each chapter of *AQA GCSE English Language Student Book 1* focuses on assessment. These units give students an opportunity to practise the skills they have developed throughout the chapter. Regular formal assessments help to monitor students' progress and assist with target-setting. Some teachers may wish to break down the assessment unit into individual activities or chunks; others may prefer to use the assessment in its entirety, to be completed under exam-type conditions, where the questions are given a set timing.

Many of the activities in this unit build up to assessment questions which echo the tasks that will be set in the exam Paper 1 or Paper 2, providing early practice of responding to exam-style questions. A summary of the relationship between the assessment units and exam paper questions can be found on pages 102–103 of this Teacher Companion.

Working through Chapter 3 'Trapped', students will be developing the essential reading and writing skills for their GCSE exam. This unit will assess whether they have grasped these skills and if they can demonstrate how to employ them in an assessment situation.

What are students demonstrating?

Reading

Students will be able to:

- identify information within a text
- summarize and compare writers' ideas
- analyse how a writer uses language and structure for effect
- evaluate what a writer does to make their writing successful.

Writing

Students will be able to:

- plan, write and proofread a letter to a newspaper, explaining a viewpoint.

How to deliver the assessment

You might wish to separate the reading and writing assessment activities into two separate lessons. Look at the questions in all of the activities and, if students are completing these under exam-type conditions, emphasize the importance of time management. A Word document version of the end of chapter assessment is available on Kerboodle which can be assigned to students.

Understanding the assessment

If necessary, allow time to discuss what is expected in the assessment activities.

Remind students to look carefully at the wording of the questions:

- If they are told to refer to a specific part of the source text, they must ensure that they do focus on that part, and not get distracted by the rest of the text.

- They should note key words used in the questions, such as 'summarize', 'compare', 'explain', 'language', 'structure' and 'character'. Emphasize that these words give a clear indication of what students should be focusing on, and how they should present their response.

- Warn students to check whether the question refers to just one source text or two.

- If the question contains bullet points, students should check that they do cover each point in their response and not just focus on the first one.

Support

Offer support when requested. The aim of the assessment activities is to familiarize students with working in exam-type conditions with time constraints and precise instructions. It is also to build each student's confidence in preparation for the real exam and to coach students on exam techniques as appropriate.

Marking

Activity 1 can be marked using the suggested answers overleaf. This could be done either by teachers or as peer/self-assessment. The longer, more evaluative tasks, for example the 'how' questions, can be marked using the 'Skills descriptors' in the relevant Paper 1 or Paper 2 AQA Specimen mark scheme on pages 107–112 of this Teacher Companion. Sample responses (at Level 2 and Level 3) with examiner comments for Activity 4d are available on Kerboodle.

Use the chart on page 103 of this Teacher Companion to identify which question in the end-of-chapter assessment relates to which exam paper question. If the assessment responses are produced under exam conditions, bear this in mind when marking the assessments. When marking the evaluative responses, you will want to mark using the 'best fit' principle, which means that not all points in the 'Skills descriptors' need to be demonstrated in order to achieve a mark in that level. Nor will those skills necessarily be used consistently throughout the response. Finally, you will need to make a judgement, based on your professional experience and using the AQA sample student responses (available on the AQA website www.aqa.org.uk), on points such as 'range', 'relevance' and 'accuracy' as used within the 'Skills descriptors' in the mark scheme.

AQA GCSE English Language Student Book 1 answers

Below are the answers to any largely non-subjective *Student Book 1* activities contained within this chapter.

Lesson 1 Survival of the fittest

Activity 1

True, False, True, False, True, False, False, True

Lesson 2 Turtle trap

Activity 1

a. clung, broken, adrift, dishwater

Lesson 4 Fighting back

Activity 1

a. 'dark street', 'high wall of the convent', 'barred door', 'waste land', 'darkness', 'wilderness of wire and iron'

Lesson 7 Time warp

Activity 1

a. Long white veil hanging from her hair; bridal flowers in her hair; bright jewels sparkled on her neck and hands, and others lay sparkling on the table

b. Paragraph 1: Half-packed trunks; one shoe on and one on the table; veil was half-arranged; watch and chain not put on; lace, handkerchief, gloves, watch, flowers and prayer book all piled up by the mirror

   Paragraph 2: the bride had withered and shrunk into a skeletal size, so the dress no longer fitted her; there was nothing bright except the feverish brightness of her sunken eyes

Lesson 8 For better or worse?

Activity 1

a. Sara didn't drink alcohol; she didn't go out clubbing; she helped run the family home after the college day had finished; she was 17 when she found her first boyfriend.

b. Sara had accepted her father's strict rules without protesting or complaining.

c. Sara expected to have more than one relationship, rather than find a life partner in her teens.

d. Focus on the word 'betrayal'.

Assessment unit

Activity 1

a. He has a widescreen TV; stereo; three meals a day; he does not have to work; he enjoys his life; he does not want to leave jail.

Chapter 4: All in the mind

Chapter overview

Why are we teaching this?

The power and scope of the human imagination is a fascinating subject, and one that has inspired writers for centuries. The focus on the individual mind and different perspectives on the world is exemplified through a wide range of texts in this chapter, including extracts from works by Sylvia Plath, Edgar Allan Poe, Erin Morganstern, Lewis Carroll, Salman Rushdie, Mary Shelley and Jonny Wilkinson.

This chapter provides many opportunities for students to develop their skills in reading and writing – with the explicit aim of using those skills effectively in the final GCSE exam. With both literary and non-fiction texts used as a basis for study, students are led to explore the nature of language used by writers and are encouraged to analyse the effect of language on readers. They are also given opportunities to plan and structure their own writing and to develop their ability to use a wider range of language features for deliberate effects on readers.

Speaking and listening tasks, ranging from paired and group discussion to role play and individual presentations, are also included in order to initiate and encourage the sharing of ideas through talk, as well as to consider the effect of language on listeners.

What are the learning aims?

The main skills and learning objectives are summarized at the start of each lesson in *AQA GCSE English Language Student Book 1*. These are all linked to aspects of the Assessment Objectives (AOs), which are also flagged at the start of each lesson.

By the end of this chapter, students will be developing all of the major skills required by the AQA English language course. They will be able to:

- read a range of texts critically in order to identify and select evidence (AO1, AO4)
- identify and interpret explicit and implicit ideas in texts (AO1)
- analyse how writers have used language and structure to achieve particular effects (AO2)
- compare how writers' ideas are conveyed across two texts (AO3)
- write imaginatively, adapting tone and style for a specific form (AO5)
- use a range of vocabulary for effect and with accuracy (AO6).

How will this be assessed?

Activities within each lesson

Teachers can choose to assess some or all of the activities within each lesson. Some activities have built-in self- and peer-assessment and these should be used in a formative way, encouraging students to monitor their own progress and increase their awareness of how to make improvements to their work.

Progress check

The second unit ends with a Progress check (on page 143), which encourages students to reflect on areas of strength and weakness in their learning. A Progress check is also available on Kerboodle, which can be adapted for differentiation. For example, more sophisticated skills can be added to the grid for the higher attainers, or more detailed basic skills can be added for students who need more support with them.

Completing the Progress checks should be followed by identification of skill areas that need more work, a plan of how to target these for further improvement and a date to monitor them again.

Assessment unit

The assessment unit focuses on the reading and writing skills covered in this chapter, and gives students the opportunity to revise and practise them in a series of activities, using source texts similar to the ones they will encounter in their exam.

Spoken Language

Teachers will need to offer opportunities for the assessment of Spoken English throughout the course. See pages 122–123 of this Teacher Companion for more information. Activities that could be developed into Spoken Language tasks have been flagged in each lesson.

Lesson sequence

Below is a suggested lesson sequence, but you might choose to alter or add to it to suit your particular teaching needs. Note that the material involved in some of the lessons outlined may be covered over two or more teaching sessions.

Introducing the chapter

- Introduce the main subject of the chapter: the power of the human mind and imagination.
- Discuss the quotation from William Blake and the outcome of the activity.
- Explore the structure of the chapter and its first two units, 'Phantasmagoria' – looking at the power of the imagination, and 'A fine line' – dealing with the fragility of the human mind.
- Outline the reading and writing skills covered in this chapter and the relevance of these skills for the final GCSE exam.

1 Talking cats	**2 Masters of the macabre**	**3 Tales of enchantment**
• Discuss talking animals in literary fiction. • Respond to the extracts from *Alice's Adventures in Wonderland* and *Coraline*. • Explore the use of description and how this affects readers' interpretations. • Select evidence from both extracts to justify opinions.	• Explore the gothic genre through extracts from *The Masque of the Red Death* and *Frankenstein*. • Analyse the effect of language features in creating mood and tone. • Compare two gothic texts.	• Explore fantasy texts, starting with an extract from *The Night Circus*. • Analyse the use of imagery, tense and narrative voice. • Prepare for writing through a word web and dramatized scene. • Write a fantasy or gothic description.
4 A bizarre start	**5 Tough at the top**	**6 Mind blowing**
• Discuss the effect of titles on readers' expectations. • Explore the impact of the opening lines of *The Enchantress of Florence*. • Focus on the structural and language features of an extract.	• Respond to an extract from the autobiography of Jonny Wilkinson. • Discuss the nature of obsession. • Select quotations from the text to support opinions. • Write a summary.	• Respond to *Confessions of an English Opium-Eater* and a contemporary text about 'legal highs'. • Analyse an anti-drugs poster in terms of imagery and language. • Compare the perspectives of two writers. • Write an article for a student newsletter.
7 Crossing the line	**8 Looking past the mirror**	**Assessment**
• Respond to an article and an extract from Sylvia Plath's journal. • Analyse different interpretations of the headline, 'Crossing the Line'. • Explore how imagery and extended metaphor convey meaning.	• Respond to Terry Pratchett's description of coping with dementia. • Analyse the way language is used for persuasive and emotive effects. • Explore changes in narrative perspective.	• Use the Progress chart on page 143 of the Student Book to assess the level of skill achieved in order to plan further action and to prioritize revision and practice. • Unit 3 revises the skills required by the reading and writing Assessment Objectives covered in the chapter and offers opportunity for further practice.

Preparing to teach

Refresh your knowledge

You might find it helpful to refer to the following key points when planning the teaching of this chapter:

- Individual characters in literary fiction have always been subject to some form of psychological analysis through the 'evidence' of their thoughts, or through dialogue. Students will have a good deal of experience of reading texts that focus on the thoughts of characters, particularly in modern young adult fiction.

- Teachers often approach imaginative writing by asking students to empathize with others by writing from their perspective. This writing may be based on characters being studied in a text or on imaginary personas.

- Writing introspectively as an 'other' will allow students to explore emotional subjects which they may not have personally experienced. This will demand a range of specific vocabulary and language features to create a sense of authenticity. Writing thoughts and feelings is often framed through a diary or journal format, although the intended audience beyond the writer should be considered.

- This is a sensitive and thought-provoking subject, because it allows the reader to see the world through the eyes of individuals who have suffered greatly from significant emotional trauma – leading to lasting psychological conditions and damage. The subject of depression is presented here through the autobiography of Jonny Wilkinson and the journal of Sylvia Plath. Though some background material is included in the lesson notes, it may be useful to research this further to find other appropriate material for a particular group of students.

Links and further reading

- For students who are interested in other examples of fantasy literature, direct them towards J. R. R. Tolkein and C. S. Lewis, or for more modern fantasy literature, towards the 'Discworld' series by Terry Pratchett and works by Neil Gaiman. Explain that the fantasy genre is a tradition that stretches back through literature from ancient Greek and Roman tales, such as the *Odyssey* and *Illiad*, through medieval folklore such as Arthurian legends, to modern literature such as the 'His Dark Materials' series, 'The Wizard of Earthsea' series and *Harry Potter*.

- Gothic novels that students may enjoy are *Dracula* by Bram Stoker, and other short stories by Edgar Allan Poe. The resurgence of interest in gothic novels in the 19th century produced stories such as *The Strange Case of Dr Jekyll and Mr Hyde* by Robert Louis Stevenson, and *The Picture of Dorian Gray* by Oscar Wilde.

- Further suggestions for gothic novels can be found in an article for Books For Keeps: http://booksforkeeps.co.uk/issue/184/childrens-books/articles/ten-of-the-best/ten-of-the-best-gothic-novels.

- It may be useful to research some other extracts from fiction texts that explore mental torment, such as *The Yellow Wallpaper* by Charlotte Perkins Gilman (which presents a married woman's mental breakdown, deemed a 'temporary nervous depression – a slight hysterical tendency', by her husband) or *Stone Cold* by Robert Swindells (where a psychotic individual is convinced that it is his duty to eradicate homeless young people from the streets).

- Further information about mental health, particularly affecting young people, is available on websites such as http://teenmentalhealth.org/learn/

- Students who are interested in the works of Sylvia Plath could be directed to her novel *The Bell Jar*, and her collections of poetry, such as *Ariel*.
- Students might be interested in reading other biographical and autobiographical accounts of high-achieving individuals in the public eye who have suffered from mental health problems, such as depression, for example Stephen Fry, Johnny Vegas and Ruby Wax.

Please note that OUP is not responsible for third-party content. Although all links were correct at the time of publication, the content and location of this material may change.

Planning guidelines and teaching tips	Think about how you can make the materials relevant to your students and responsive to their particular needs and learning targets. Some suggested approaches to address key areas are provided below.

- You should be aware of all students' **prior performance and targets** for the end of year or course. It may be useful to include this information (perhaps colour-coded) on a seating plan. In this way it will be easier to reseat students in different groups based on ability — whether for particular grades or a range for support.
- Think carefully about **groupings**. For instance, it may benefit students who have collaborated on a previous task, analysing a writer's use of language, to work together again to build on the former learning and develop their skills.
- Draw upon **students' wider reading** wherever possible, even if referring back to texts that they read when they were younger, for example when discussing the role of animals in children's literature generally. Also encourage further reading stimulated by extracts featured in this chapter (see some recommendations above), to build up their knowledge of particular **literary genres** and how they develop through different eras.
- Offer lots of **support** with reading texts such as *Frankenstein* and *Confessions of an English Opium-Eater*, where the lexical density of the language is more challenging due to the **historical context** of the production.
- Make sure that students are not intimidated by sharing their ideas with others and encourage them to **self- and peer-assess** — especially when dealing with imaginative writing. Students will learn from **modelling** — do not be afraid to write in front of students yourself, making mistakes and changing your mind as you work towards a more polished response.
- Some of the extracts in this chapter could create challenges for **more reluctant readers**, as well as **EAL** students. Be prepared to work with these students in one-to-one and guided group contexts to support their reading. Consider strategies to keep their interest and build their reading stamina, such as quick comprehension quizzes to add an element of competition to their reading.
- Refer to the **Grammar Reference Guide** on Kerboodle for definitions and examples of specific grammatical features covered by this chapter.
- Plan carefully for differentiation, using the **Support and Stretch activities** in the Student Book, and the additional ideas offered in the individual lesson support sections in this Teacher Companion.

Lesson focus

Preparation and resources
- Student Book 1, pages 118–121
- Kerboodle worksheets:
  - 4.1 Talking animals
  - 4.1 All about the cat
  - 4.1 All about Alice

What this lesson teaches and how

This lesson develops interpretation skills by asking students to explore their personal responses to the literary depiction of talking cats. Both chosen texts, *Alice's Adventures in Wonderland* by Lewis Carroll (1886) and *Coraline* by Neil Gaiman (2002), allow the characters of the cats to show the confidence and poise that is lacking in the young female protagonists who question them. Students will analyse the texts in order to identify explicit and implicit ideas presented in the dialogue as well as discussing the writers' intentions through their descriptive language.

Skills and objectives

The following skills and Assessment Objectives (AOs) are addressed in this lesson:
- To identify and interpret explicit and implicit ideas (AO1)
- To select and synthesize evidence from different texts (AO1)

Specification links

Paper 1, Section A, Question 1*
Paper 1, Section B, Question 5*

*Note that Paper 1 will not include a 19th-century fiction text (such as *Alice's Adventures in Wonderland*), but the skills developed here are transferable to any text.

1 Talking cats

Fictional animals

Before the lesson, give students the 'Talking animals' worksheet and ask them to prepare some ideas about talking animals they have encountered in literary fiction, on children's TV or in films.

In the lesson, use the above preparation for a discussion activity, with a particular focus on the reasons why talking animals have been used by a range of writers over time. This could be extended into a full presentation.

Resources
Kerboodle: 4.1 Talking animals worksheet

Spoken Language opportunity

Character references

Ensure students understand the difference between explicit and implicit information, and can interpret what a writer is implying through their choice of language. Use the 'All about the cat' worksheet to help students record their ideas for Activity 1.

Resources
Student Book 1: Activity 1, page 118
Kerboodle: 4.1 All about the cat worksheet

What do we learn about Alice?

The 'All about Alice' worksheet will support students in recognizing the difference between explicit and implicit information. You may wish to add more detail and examples to the grid for students who need a higher level of support.

Resources
Student Book 1: Activity 2, page 119
Kerboodle: 4.1 All about Alice worksheet

Support

Dialogue and adverbs

Discuss how the use of adverbs gives clues about the personality of the characters in the extract. Encourage students to write their own dialogue, including adverbs that suggest certain characteristics about the child and animal they are describing. Invite students to role-play their dialogue, using body language, facial expression and tone to convey their character accurately according to their descriptions.

Resources
Student Book 1: Activity 3, page 121

Which one would you like to meet?

To extend Activity 4, place students in groups to discuss which of the two fictional cats they would like to meet. Each group should report to the class with clear evidence for their choice. Previous notes should support the discussions. This may conclude that the choice is about which cat is least objectionable!

Resources
Student Book 1: Activity 4, page 121

Characteristics associated with animals

Ask students to research the characteristics usually associated with the depiction of particular animals in literature. For example, encourage them to look at the portrayal of a fox in the 'Nun's Priest's Tale' by Geoffrey Chaucer, and to compare its behaviour with other foxes in literature. Clearly, its devious and cunning traits can be seen in lots of folk tales and fables. Other groups could research the depiction of animals such as the wolf or lion.

Stretch

Lesson focus

Preparation and resources

- Student Book 1, pages 122–127
- Kerboodle worksheets:
  - 4.2 The effect of language features
  - 4.2 Mary Shelley
  - 4.2 Bringing horror to life

What this lesson teaches and how

Students are introduced to two writers of the gothic tradition: Edgar Allan Poe and Mary Shelley. The extracts from *The Masque of the Red Death* (1842) and *Frankenstein* (1818) are focused upon in terms of the writers' evocative use of vocabulary, language features and sentence structure in order to powerfully and dramatically affect the reader's imagination. Students will be led to understand how writing can affect the reader, and to compare the methods adopted by the writers in order to convey their ideas.

Skills and objectives

The following skills and Assessment Objectives (AOs) are addressed in this lesson:

- To analyse how writers use language to create effects (AO2)
- To compare how writers' ideas are conveyed across two texts (AO3)

Specification links

Paper 1, Section A, Question 2*
Paper 2, Section A, Question 4**

*Note that Paper 1 will not include a 19th-century fiction text (such as *The Masque of the Red Death*), but the skills developed here are transferable to any text.
**Likewise, in Paper 2, students will be comparing two non-fiction texts, rather than one fiction and one non-fiction (as in this lesson), but the skills developed here are transferable.

2 Masters of the macabre

Describing scary places

Before the lesson, ask students to write a description of a scary place in 50 words. You could give them a choice of titles, such as 'The Walk Home', 'The Empty House' or 'The Old Church'. Encourage them to think carefully about the power and effect of the words, language features and sentence structure within their description. At the start of the lesson, students should share their writing in groups and choose the best features, to be shared with the whole class.

Comparing writing with film

After analysing the effects and connotations of language in the Poe extract in Activity 1, display some images from the 1964 Vincent Price film (or other productions which suit the class most appropriately). Group students and ask them to discuss the images and to select the one which most relates to the images they visualized when reading the text. Discussions should relate to colours and textures and then link to the power of written language.

Resources

Student Book 1: Activity 1, page 123

Graphic image

As an alternative to making a collage (Support for Activity 2) ask students to draw or paint their own image – possibly abstract – presenting their impressions of the scene described by Poe. Encourage them to explain how they have been inspired by specific language used in the text.

Resources

Student Book 1: Activity 2 page 123

The effect of language features

Use the 'Effect of language features' worksheet on Kerboodle to provide students with a grid to help them respond to Activity 3. You may wish to add some examples to support less confident students. Gather ideas from around the class at the end of the activity to allow all the ideas to be shared, discussed and noted.

Resources

Student Book 1: Activity 3, page 124
Kerboodle: 4.2 The effect of language features worksheet

Mary Shelley

In Activity 4, students are asked to read the introduction to *Frankenstein* where Mary Shelley reflects upon her childhood imagination and her enjoyment of creating stories. Students are asked to focus upon the meaning and effect of specific words and phrases. Some support in structuring answers is offered on the Kerboodle worksheet, plus some additional questions.

Resources

Student Book 1: Activity 4, page 125
Kerboodle: 4.2 Mary Shelley worksheet

Support

Bringing horror to life

Give more able students the extract from *Frankenstein* on the Kerboodle worksheet, and ask them to explore how the author uses language to convey Frankenstein's horror and disgust at the monster he has created.

Resources

Kerboodle: 4.2 Bringing horror to life worksheet

Stretch

Lesson focus

Preparation and resources
- Student Book 1, pages 128–129
- Kerboodle worksheets:
  - 4.3 The use of senses in description
  - 4.3 Writing in a chosen style

What this lesson teaches and how

Students are introduced to an extract from *The Night Circus* by Erin Morgenstern (2011). There is a development from previous lessons in the unit where language features and their effects on readers are identified, analysed and practised. Students will also be able to develop their own use of language for specific effects on an audience. The main task is to write in a convincing enchanted or gothic style, based on features of the texts read in Lessons 2 and 3. Support for students in understanding terms and ideas is given in the Student Book.

Skills and objectives

The following skills and Assessment Objectives (AOs) are addressed in this lesson:
- To communicate imaginatively, adapting tone and style for a specific form (AO5)
- To use a range of vocabulary for effect and with accuracy (AO6)

Specification link

Paper 1, Section B, Question 5

3 Tales of enchantment

Researching fantasy texts

Before the lesson, ask students to think about stories they read as younger children, or any of their current reading, that may be classified as 'fantasy'. They should be able to offer some justification as to why they may be seen as 'fantasy' texts. In class, encourage group discussion leading to a shared understanding of 'fantasy criteria'. (See 'Writing in the fantasy genre' below.)

Using the senses in description

After reading the extract from *The Night Circus*, ask students to work in pairs to find examples of imagery appealing to different senses and used to evoke particular feelings and ideas in the reader. Encourage them to discuss their findings and note them down on the 'Use of senses in description' worksheet on Kerboodle.

Resources

Student Book 1: Extract from *The Night Circus*, page 128
Kerboodle: 4.3 The use of senses in description worksheet

Language features

In Activity 1, students consider how the writer uses language features such as narrative voice, alliteration, imagery and tense to engage the imagination of the reader. Challenge higher attaining students to decide which features have the most powerful effect in creating the sense of enchantment or fantasy in the text.

Resources

Student Book 1: Activity 1, page 128

Stretch

Sharing word webs

Activity 2 could be adapted to a group activity, where students are given particular vocabulary associated with fantasy or gothic literature to explore through word webs. They could start with words such as shadows, moon, terror, land, journey, quest, challenge, gateway, but then encourage them to come up with their own words to explore and share between groups.

Resources

Student Book 1: Activity 2, page 129

SPAG

Writing in the fantasy genre

If students choose to write in the fantasy genre, remind them that key features of the genre include some of the following: magic, witchcraft, mythical creatures or talking animals, another planet or another dimension of this world, heroes and heroines battling dark forces. Note that science fiction is different in that it is based on futuristic technological advances.

Remind students that their description should evoke a very strong sense of place and atmosphere, so their language choices should evoke powerful imaginative pictures for the reader.

Writing in a chosen style

For students who need additional support with getting started, use the 'Writing in a chosen style' worksheet on Kerboodle. Encourage students to adopt one of the ideas and styles and develop it as their own, or use them simply to stimulate further ideas. Note that there are a variety of examples of narrative voice, tense, mood and tone.

Resources

Student Book 1: Activity 4, page 129
Kerboodle: 4.3 Writing in a chosen style worksheet

Support

Lesson focus

Preparation and resources

- Student Book 1, pages 130–131
- Kerboodle worksheets:
  - 4.4 Setting the scene
  - 4.4 A bizarre start
  - 4.4 Writing an evaluation

What this lesson teaches and how

This lesson analyses the structure of a text in some detail, from the title to the development of information through the first paragraph. Students are guided to reflect on the use of structure to alter the focus and perspective of the reader. Close textual analysis is being practised here, based on the development of some language skills from previous lessons in the chapter.

Skills and objectives

The following skills and Assessment Objectives (AOs) are addressed in this lesson:

- To analyse how writers use structure to achieve effects (AO2)
- To evaluate texts critically and select evidence (AO4)

Specification link

Paper 1, Section A, Question 3 and 4

4 A bizarre start

Intriguing titles

As a warm-up activity, give each student a sticky note and ask them to write down the title of the most intriguing book they have read or heard about. All notes should be attached to a central place, then each student chooses a different title and explains what they imagine the text is about. (Encourage students to choose titles that they are unfamiliar with.)

Resources

Sticky notes for students to write on

The effect of a title

For Activity 1, students can be organized into pairs or larger groups in order to discuss the effect of the title *The Enchantress of Florence*. Drawing on the previous activity suggested above, students should have a wide series of terms to use in discussing their ideas. Feedback could be managed by random name selection for initial views, then select students to comment on the ideas of others.

Resources

Student Book 1: Activity 1, page 130

Spoken Language opportunity

Setting the scene

To emphasize the importance and impact of the first line of a text, use the 'Setting the scene' worksheet on Kerboodle. Ask students what they can deduce about the time, setting and possible genre of the ten story openings. The discussion should lead to deeper thinking about the scene being described and the implications of the language choice on the reader.

Resources

Kerboodle: 4.4 Setting the scene worksheet

Structuring the text analysis

When analysing the structural features of the extract, you may wish to assign different sections to different groups, then ask them to feed back to the rest of the class. Alternatively, envoys from each group could be sent to find out what other groups have decided in order to report back. This strategy increases student responsibility and the need to communicate clearly. The worksheet on Kerboodle can be used to provide support.

Resources

Student Book 1: Activity 2, page 131
Kerboodle: 4.4 A bizarre start worksheet

Writing an evaluation

For students who need additional support, use the 'Writing an Evaluation' worksheet on Kerboodle to help students complete the main activity based on the learning and research in the lesson. Remind students of their earlier writing about texts and the need to use quotations in order to support their ideas.

Resources

Student Book 1: Activity 3, page 131
Kerboodle: 4.4 Writing an evaluation worksheet

Support

Lesson focus

Preparation and resources

- Student Book 1, pages 132–133
- Kerboodle worksheets:
  - 4.5 Reflections on feelings
  - 4.5 Selecting and justifying quotations
  - 4.5 Writing a summary

What this lesson teaches and how

Jonny Wilkinson, the famous England rugby union international player, is the main focus of this lesson – through the analysis of his reflections on depression in his autobiography. Through his own description of his mental state, students will not only gain an insight into what makes a champion but will also see how powerful writing can make an emotional connection with the reader. They will also practise finding evidence in a text to support their ideas.

Skills and objectives

The following skills and Assessment Objectives (AOs) are addressed in this lesson:
- To identify and interpret implicit ideas (AO1)
- To select evidence from texts (AO1)

Specification link

Paper 2, Section A, Questions 1 and 2

5 Tough at the top

Reflections on feelings

In preparation for the lesson, ask students to think about a range of feelings and emotions they have experienced about their achievements and school life. Give them the 'Reflections on feelings' worksheet on Kerboodle to record their thoughts. Naturally this would need to be planned with some awareness of students' experiences but it should yield some thoughtful and sensitive writing. Encourage students to share their work in small groups.

Resources

Kerboodle: 4.5 Reflections on feelings worksheet

Obsession

To support Activity 1, ask students if they have a passion, such as Jonny Wilkinson's passion for rugby. Discuss how a passion can become an obsession and how you would recognize this extreme. Draw out the difference between attention to detail to improve performance, and an overwhelming drive to be the best, to the exclusion of all else. This discussion should help students to understand Jonny Wilkinson's state of mind as recounted in the text.

Resources

Student Book 1: Activity 1, page 133

Grabbing attention

After drawing attention to the lesson's title 'Tough at the top', ask higher achieving students how appropriate they think it is for the content of this lesson, and to explain their opinion. Then ask them to think of an alternative title, which would be equally appropriate, concise and to the point. Encourage them to explain the rationale of their new title.

Stretch

Identifying appropriate quotations

Give out the worksheet 'Selecting and justifying quotations' from Kerboodle, to support students in completing Activity 2. Emphasize that short quotations – often just a few words or phrases – are the best choices, rather than longer, complete sentences.

Resources

Student Book 1: Activity 2a and 2b, page 133
Kerboodle: 4.5 Selecting and justifying quotations worksheet

Writing a summary

For students who need additional support, use the 'Writing a summary' worksheet on Kerboodle to help students complete the main activity based on the learning and research in the lesson. This gives support in structuring a summary of the key points in the text. Remind students to include quotations in order to support their ideas.

Resources

Student Book 1: Activity 2c, page 133
Kerboodle: 4.5 Writing a summary worksheet

Support

Lesson focus

Preparation and resources
- Student Book 1, pages 134–137
- Kerboodle worksheet:
  - 4.6 Comparing writers' methods

What this lesson teaches and how

This lesson deals with some challenging material, with an extract from Thomas de Quincey's *Confessions of an English Opium-Eater* (1821) and a contemporary non-fiction text dealing with 'legal highs'. Students will compare the way the two writers present their respective messages to the reader. Then they will plan, write and proofread an article of their own on the same theme.

Skills and objectives

The following skills and Assessment Objectives (AOs) are addressed in this lesson:
- To compare writers' perspectives and how these are conveyed (AO3)
- To write for different purposes, forms and audiences, organizing ideas (AO5)

Specification links

Paper 2, Section A, Question 4
Paper 2, Section B, Question 5

6 Mind blowing

Key words

The taking of recreational drugs has long been a taboo subject in society. However, students should be well aware of the dangers from previous school sessions and direct or secondary personal experience. Ask groups of students to compile a list of ten words linked to the subject of the dangers of drug-taking, before reading any texts in this lesson. This activity could be developed into a Spoken Language presentation.

Spoken Language opportunity

Campaign materials

Display some anti-drug campaign materials. Ask students to discuss the effectiveness of images and texts on the audience. Encourage them to think in detail about the impact of vocabulary, statements, punctuation and visuals, in conveying the message.

Resources

Key in 'anti-drug public service announcements' into a search engine, and you should access some relevant short videos

Analysing perspectives

If students need more support to complete Activity 3, give them the 'Comparing writers' methods' worksheet on Kerboodle. Students should use the worksheet to plan their writing. Depending on the level of support required, you may wish to add more detail to the worksheet in terms of sentence starters, vocabulary and quotations.

Resources

Student Book 1: Activity 3, page 136
Kerboodle: 4.6 Comparing writers' methods worksheet

Support

Writing a radio script

Challenge pairs of students to write a short snappy commercial about the dangers of drugs, using a scripted scene to highlight a point. Remind them to think carefully about their intended audience (i.e. teenagers) and how they can convey their message in a memorable way, clearly explaining the dangers.

Writing an article

Ask higher attaining students to write for a more challenging audience, such as parents or teachers. Clearly, this has implications for the content, language, structure and tone of the text. Students should research other texts closely before planning how they should most appropriately and effectively present their ideas.

Remind all students to proofread their work carefully. If they need SPAG revision, refer to the Grammar Reference Guide.

Resources

Student Book 1: Activity 4, page 137

Stretch

Lesson focus

Preparation and resources
- Student Book 1, pages 138–141
- Weblink: www.bio.com
- Kerboodle worksheet:
  - 4.7 A complicated mind

What this lesson teaches and how

The two texts studied in this lesson deal with the subject of mental illness, but from very different perspectives. They present students with some challenging material in terms of both the subject matter and also in the analysis and deconstruction of the texts. Students will be asked to identify explicit information taken from the texts, as well as interpreting and understanding implicit ideas with supporting references.

Skills and objectives

The following skills and Assessment Objectives (AOs) are addressed in this lesson:
- To identify explicit information and interpret implicit ideas, and to summarize evidence from different texts (AO1)
- To analyse how writers use language to achieve effects (AO2)

Specification link

Paper 2, Section A, Questions 1, 2 and 3

7 Crossing the line

Memory loss

After reading the first text, challenge students to think how they would view their present life if they had their memory wiped of the last four years (e.g. the whole of their secondary school life so far). This could be written in a diary format with the aim of showing the strangeness of what now is familiar.

Resources

Student Book 1: Extract 'Rare amnesia…', page 138

Sharing responses

Following on from the previous task, students should share their diary responses with at least four other students. Students should give feedback to each other about the way they have expressed their feelings and the interesting ways in which they have described things that are 'unfamiliar'. This should lead to some intriguing and amusing ideas as students share some of their best 'finds' from around the room.

Interpreting the title

Draw attention to the title of the lesson and ask students to think about why it has been chosen. 'Crossing the line' may have different connotations to students ranging from a literal understanding of physically crossing a line (in a race perhaps) to a more metaphorical understanding of the term.

A complicated mind

Use the worksheet 'A complicated mind' on Kerboodle to support students in responding to Activity 2. You may wish to complete one or more examples for lower attaining students. Ask higher attaining students to add more quotations to the grid and more descriptions from Sylvia Plath, drawing on material from the extract.

Resources

Student Book 1: Activity 2, page 140
Kerboodle: 4.7 A complicated mind worksheet

Support and stretch

Sylvia Plath – background

Information and short biographical films dealing with Plath's struggles with mental illness can be found on www.biography.com.

Resources

Weblink: http://www.biography.com/people/sylvia-plath-9442550#synopsis

Using quotations

In Activities 3 and 4 ensure that students are confident about how to incorporate quotations into their writing. Emphasize that the quotations can be just key words and phrases, as well as longer extracts. Remind students to explain the quotations and their effects, rather than just identifying them. Encourage students to talk through their ideas and explanations before writing them down.

Resources

Student Book 1: Activities 3 and 4, page 141

Lesson focus

8 Looking past the mirror

Preparation and resources

- Student Book 1, pages 142–143
- Kerboodle worksheets:
  - 4.8 Fighting for a cause
  - 4.8 Language for emotive effect
  - 4.8 Progress check

What this lesson teaches and how

The final lesson in this section focuses on the famous writer Terry Pratchett, who campaigned to highlight the condition of dementia since it did effect him personally. His account of the way that he had to learn to live with dementia is a powerful piece of writing. This will give students plenty of evidence for identifying and evaluating the effect of language and structural features, as well as developing their own skills of expression and explanation.

Skills and objectives

The following skills and Assessment Objectives (AOs) are addressed in this lesson:

- To analyse how writers use language and structure to create effects (AO2)
- To evaluate texts and support with evidence (AO4)

Specification links

Paper 1, Section A, Question 4
Paper 2, Section A, Question 3*

*Note that AO4 is not specifically tested in Paper 2 (which focuses on non-fiction texts), but the skills are transferable to fiction texts, which will feature in Paper 1.

Fighting for a cause

Ask students to think about promoting a cause or issue, such as a charity or an argument that is current, e.g. criticism of young people using too much I.T. in their daily lives. The worksheet 'Fighting for a cause' on Kerboodle can help with planning and remind students of the key features of a persuasive text. This can be peer-assessed, and the best chosen for sharing.

Resources

Kerboodle: 4.8 Fighting for a cause worksheet

Addressing an audience

Students can develop a presentation based on their persuasive writing done in the activity above. Remind them that this task has the same aim as the writing task, i.e. they have to engage others and persuade them through the way they present their ideas. Remind students to think about delivery in terms of clarity of diction, volume, pace, tone, body language and eye contact with the audience. They should be prepared to answer questions after their presentation.

Resources

Prior work on 'Fighting for a cause'

Spoken Language opportunity

Using language for emotive effect

Use the worksheet 'Language for emotive effect' on Kerboodle to support students in responding to Activity 1. You could add more sentence starters and examples depending on the extent of support that your students need. Some may find it helpful to rehearse their answers orally with a partner first, before completing the grid.

Resources

Student Book 1: Activity 1, page 142
Kerboodle: 4.8 Language for emotive effect worksheet

Support

What would you do?

This chapter has highlighted many cases of suffering through mental health issues. Ask students to think about how they would try to alleviate some of that suffering if they were in charge of some funding. Ask groups to plan how they would spend one million pounds, in order to help people with mental health problems. If they need prompts, encourage them to think about charities, funding for drugs, developing public awareness campaigns, etc.

Progress check

Give students copies of the Progress check worksheet on Kerboodle and ask them to evaluate the progress of their skills after studying the texts in the chapter and completing the activities.

Resources

Student Book 1: Progress check, page 143
Kerboodle: 4.8 Progress check worksheet

Unit 3: Assessment

Assessment Objectives

All six reading and writing Assessment Objectives (AOs) are addressed in this unit (AO1, AO2, AO3, AO4, AO5, AO6).

Why do we have an assessment unit?

The final unit in each chapter of *AQA GCSE English Language Student Book 1* focuses on assessment. These units give students an opportunity to practise the skills they have developed throughout the chapter. Regular formal assessments help to monitor students' progress and assist with target-setting. Some teachers may wish to break down the assessment unit into individual activities or chunks; others may prefer to use the assessment in its entirety, to be completed under exam-type conditions where the questions are given a set timing.

Many of the activities in this unit build up to assessment questions which echo the tasks that will be set in the exam Paper 1 or Paper 2, providing early practice of responding to exam-style units. A summary of the relationship between the assessment units and exam paper questions can be found on pages 102–103 of this Teacher Companion.

While working through Chapter 4, 'All in the mind', students will be developing the essential reading and writing skills for their GCSE exam. This unit assesses whether they have grasped these skills and if they can demonstrate how to employ them in an assessment situation.

What are students demonstrating?

Reading

Students will be able to:

- Identify and interpret information within a text
- summarize and compare writers' ideas
- analyse how a writer uses language and structure for effect
- evaluate what a writer does to make their writing successful.

Writing

Students will be able to:

- plan, write and proofread a persuasive article for a newspaper about attitudes towards old people.

How to deliver the assessment

You might wish to separate the reading and writing assessment activities into two separate lessons. Look at the questions in all of the activities and, if students are completing these under exam-type conditions, emphasize the importance of time management. A Word document version of the end of chapter assessment is available on Kerboodle which can be assigned to students.

Understanding the assessment

If necessary, allow time to discuss what is expected in the assessment activities.

Remind students to look carefully at the wording of the questions:

- If they are told to refer to a specific part of the source text, they must ensure that they do focus on that part, and not get distracted by the rest of the text.

- They should note key words used in the questions, such as 'summarize', 'compare', 'explain', 'language', 'structure' and 'character'. Emphasize that these words give a clear indication of what students should be focusing on, and how they should present their response.

- Warn students to check whether the question refers to just one source text or two.

- If the question contains bullet points, students should check that they do cover each point in their response and not just focus on the first one.

Support

Offer support when requested. The aim of the assessment activities is to familiarize students with working in exam-type conditions with time constraints and precise instructions. It is also to build each student's confidence in preparation for the real exam and to coach students on exam techniques as appropriate.

Marking

Activity 1 and Activity 4 can be marked using the suggested answers overleaf. This could be done either by teachers or as peer/self-assessment. The longer, more evaluative tasks, for example the 'how' questions, can be marked using the 'Skills descriptors' in the relevant Paper 1 or Paper 2 AQA Specimen mark scheme on pages 107–112 of this Teacher Companion. Sample responses (at Level 1 and Level 3) with examiner comments for Activity 6 are available on Kerboodle.

Use the chart on page 103 of this Teacher Companion to identify which question in the end-of-chapter assessment relates to which exam paper question. If the assessment responses are produced under exam conditions, bear this in mind when marking the assessments. When marking the evaluative responses, you will want to mark using the 'best fit' principle, which means that not all points in the 'Skills descriptors' need to be demonstrated in order to achieve a mark in that level. Nor will those skills necessarily be used consistently throughout the response. Finally, you will need to make a judgement, based on your professional experience and using the AQA sample student responses (available on the AQA website www.aqa.org.uk), on points such as 'range', 'relevance' and 'accuracy' as used within the 'Skills descriptors' in the mark scheme

AQA GCSE English Language Student Book 1 answers

Below are the answers to any largely non-subjective *Student Book 1* activities contained within this chapter.

Lesson 1 Talking cats

Activity 1

a. The cat was sitting on a tree branch; it could smile; it seemed to respond to Alice's address; it had long claws; it had many teeth; it looked good-natured.

Activity 2

a. Alice is inquisitive; she does not think it unusual to converse with a cat; she is polite and respectful; she is intelligent for her age – she is able to discuss the most appropriate verbs.

Activity 3

a. *smoothly* – calm/effortless;
   drily – ironic;
   thoughtfully – intelligent;
   slowly – patient/controlling;
   carefully – self-aware;
   cattily – provocative

Lesson 2 Masters of the macabre

Activity 1

scarlet – link to death/blood;
profusion of golden ornaments – great wealth;
multitude of gaudy and fantastic appearances – a sense of unreality/fantasy;
blood tinted panes – a sense of horror/the macabre

Activity 3

a. *repetition* – 'There were much';
   personification – 'the dreams – writhed in and about/stalked';
   juxtaposition – 'all is still, and all is silent';
     symbolism – 'ebony clock/tinted windows';
   change in tenses – 'there were much/might have excited/there strikes/all is still/the music swells/dreams live';
   varied sentence forms – various examples

Lesson 5 Tough at the top

Activity 1

b. He is particularly harsh when judging himself at all times and probably never feels able to meet his own high standards.

c. He feels that his obsessive behaviour controls his life.

d. At times, he feels unable to control his obsessions and cannot put them aside.

e. He cannot respond to his emotions other than through screaming under water – he cannot talk about it.

Activity 2

Unsettled ' – and I am at home not doing anything';
Self-critical 'my own harsh judgement';
Depressed 'Everything feels pointless';
Perfectionist 'doing whatever is required to get there';
Out of control 'then I let out a scream of total frustration'

Lesson 6 Mind blowing

Activity 1

a. Possible choices: 'nightly spectacles'; 'chasms and sunless abysses'; 'utter darkness'; 'gloomy melancholy'

Lesson 7 Crossing the line

Activity 1

A. False (falling asleep in her bunk)

B. True

C. False (it was a 17-year memory gap)

D. True

E. False (we know it was stress, but not the cause of it)

F. True

G. True

H. False (she did not recognize herself)

Activity 2

a. *'the groaning inner voice'* – she was always depressed and full of self-doubt;

'I have a good self, that loves skies, hills, ideas, tasty meals, bright colors' – she was aware of a positive side to life but was not always able to think positively because the negative and pessimistic side dominated;

'It wants me to think I'm so good I must be perfect' – she can never be satisfied because her depression will always find fault with being less than perfect;

'kicking my demon down when it comes up' – she has to be constantly aware that she must suppress the negative thoughts.

b. 'I can learn to be a better teacher'; 'I am, on the contrary, something'; 'has more trouble than most facing people easily'.

Lesson 8 Looking past the mirror

Activity 1

- *'struggling to follow conversations'* – this helps the reader to understand the nature of the condition and the way it gradually separates the sufferer from normal life; this could make the reader feel uncomfortable and sympathetic.

- *'manic modern days of ours'* – suggests why we may not find time to help but strikes guilt in the reader, who may be a little more thoughtful in future.

- *'talented scientists beaver away'* – there is a great deal of work going on in the background to combat the condition from a scientific perspective, unseen to us all.

- *'hundreds of thousands of us out there'* – this number is likely to shock the reader.

Activity 2

a. The definition makes the reader focus on the damage to the brain itself before moving on to the effect on someone's life. The technical terms emphasize that dementia is a physical process of deterioration.

b. *'the campaign holds a mirror up to us all'* – this metaphor makes the reader look in at themselves and 'reflect' upon what they can do to help others dealing with the condition.

Assessment unit

Activity 1

a. The hospital is secure; visitors are not allowed to take phones into Broadmoor; it is very hard to get in – or out; it is a prison-hospital for people with severe mental disorders who are dangerous to the community and themselves.

Activity 4

b. Pity/sympathetic – *'the treatment of these unfortunates'*;

impressed – *'elegant, spacious, well-ventilated and attractive building'*;

thankful – *'a long breath of relief'*

Chapter overview

Why are we teaching this?

The effect of our immediate environment on our thoughts and feelings, and the way the 'spirit of place' can affect our perspective on the world, is the main subject of this chapter. The focus is intensified by the clear differentiation between the urban and the rural in the wide range of texts in the chapter, including extracts from works by Sir Arthur Conan Doyle, Stella Gibson, Raymond Chandler, Ross Raisin, Sylvia Plath, Laurie Lee and Thomas Hardy.

This chapter provides many opportunities for students to develop their skills in reading and writing – with the explicit aim of using those skills effectively in the final GCSE exam. With both literary fiction and non-fiction texts used as a basis for study in looking at the description of place, students are led to explore the nature of language used by writers, and are encouraged to analyse the effect of language on readers. They are also given further opportunities to plan and structure their own writing and to develop their ability to use a wider range of language features for deliberate effects on readers.

Speaking and listening tasks ranging from paired and group discussion to role play and individual presentations are also included in order to initiate and encourage the sharing of ideas through talk, as well as to consider the effect of language on listeners. Opportunities to practise and evaluate Spoken Language presentations have been embedded in many lessons.

What are the learning aims?

The main skills and learning objectives are summarized at the start of each lesson in *AQA GCSE English Language Student Book 1*. These are all linked to aspects of the Assessment Objectives (AOs), which are also flagged at the start of each lesson.

By the end of this chapter, students will be developing all of the major skills required by the AQA English language course. They will be able to:

- read a range of texts critically in order to identify and select evidence (AO1, AO4)
- identify and interpret explicit and implicit ideas in texts (AO1)
- analyse how writers have used language and structure to achieve particular effects (AO2)
- compare how writers' ideas are conveyed across two texts (AO3)
- write imaginatively, adapting tone and style for a specific form (AO5)
- use a range of vocabulary for effect and with accuracy (AO6).

How will this be assessed?

Activities within each lesson

Teachers can choose to assess some or all of the activities within each lesson. Some activities have built-in self- and peer-assessment and these should be used in a formative way, encouraging students to monitor their own progress and increase their awareness of how to make improvements to their work.

Progress check

The second unit ends with a Progress check (on page 177), which encourages students to reflect on areas of strength and weakness in their learning. A Progress check is also available on Kerboodle, which can be adapted for differentiation. For example, more sophisticated skills can be added to the grid for the higher attainers, or more detailed basic skills can be added for students who need more support with them.

Completing the Progress checks should be followed by identification of skill areas that need more work, a plan of how to target these for further improvement and a date to monitor them again.

Assessment unit

The assessment unit focuses on the reading and writing skills covered in the chapter, and gives students the opportunity to revise and practise them in a series of activities, using source texts similar to the ones that they will encounter in their exam.

Spoken Language

Teachers will need to offer opportunities for the assessment of Spoken English throughout the course. See pages 122–123 of this Teacher Companion for more information. Activities that could be developed into Spoken Language tasks have been flagged in each lesson.

Lesson sequence

Below is a suggested lesson sequence, but you might choose to alter or add to it to suit your particular teaching needs. Note that the material involved in some of the lessons outlined may be covered over two or more teaching sessions.

Introducing the chapter

- Introduce the main subject of the chapter: the description of places and the ability of writers to transport readers' minds through skilful use of language and structure.
- Discuss the pros and cons of urban and rural life, and where students would live if given the choice.
- Explore the structure of the chapter and its first two units, 'A novel setting' – analysing the power of description of place, and 'People and places' – exploring the effect of places on individuals.
- Outline the reading and writing skills covered in the chapter and the relevance of these skills for the final GCSE exam.

---

1 Brick Lane	**2 Mean streets**	**3 Rambling into danger**
<ul><li>Respond to the extract from *Brick Lane* by Monica Ali, identifying explicit and implicit information.</li><li>Use quotations to back up interpretations.</li><li>Identify the influence of narrative perspectives in the extract.</li></ul>	<ul><li>Respond to the extracts from *The Sign of Four* by Sir Arthur Conan Doyle, *Farewell My Lovely* by Raymond Chandler and *Loss* by Tony Black.</li><li>Analyse the connotations of particular words and phrases used in the extracts.</li><li>Explore skills involved in creating characters and settings.</li></ul>	<ul><li>Respond to an extract from *God's Own Country* by Ross Raisin.</li><li>Discuss the nature of humour from an abstract perspective before looking at humour in the extract.</li><li>Explore how structural features of the text influence the reader.</li></ul>
4 Tales from the dairy	**5 Sounds of the city**	**6 Trafalgar Square**
<ul><li>Respond to extracts from *Tess of the d'Urbervilles* and *Cold Comfort Farm*.</li><li>Explore onomatopoeia and symbolism.</li><li>Analyse the effects of structure on a narrative.</li><li>Plan, write and proofread a narrative with a strong sense of setting.</li></ul>	<ul><li>Respond to extracts from texts written in different centuries dealing with the invasion of personal privacy in city life.</li><li>Summarize the way sounds are described in the texts.</li><li>Compare the attitudes of the writers.</li><li>Write an article arguing a point of view.</li></ul>	<ul><li>Respond to two texts that describe Trafalgar Square.</li><li>Explore and summarize the similarities and differences between the two accounts.</li><li>Plan, write and proofread a vivid description of a place.</li></ul>
7 Selling the air	**8 The pig issue**	**Assessment**
<ul><li>Respond to an extract from 'An Obstinate Exile' by Laurie Lee.</li><li>Find evidence to demonstrate the writer's perspective.</li><li>Plan, write and proofread a description or a narrative using an image as a stimulus.</li></ul>	<ul><li>Respond to two texts written in different centuries offering diverse portrayals of pigs.</li><li>Analyse different sources of humour.</li><li>Compare how the writers use humour.</li></ul>	<ul><li>Use the Progress chart on page 177 of the Student Book to assess the level of skill achieved in order to plan further action and to prioritize revision and practice.</li><li>Unit 3 revises the skills required by the reading and writing Assessment Objectives covered in the chapter and offers opportunity for further practice.</li></ul>

Preparing to teach

Refresh your knowledge

You might find it helpful to refer to the following key points when planning the teaching of this chapter:

- The study of *Brick Lane* by Monica Ali could be supplemented by extracts from *The Buddha of Suburbia* by Hanif Kureishi, or some selected scenes from the 1999 film *East is East* by Ayub Khan-Din, which give other perspectives on coming to terms with life in Great Britain. Both texts deal with the clash between generations about what is and is not acceptable in terms of integration of culture.

- You may wish to look further into the crime fiction genre, using modern writers such as Sara Paretsky (creator of the VI Warshawski novels) or Ian Rankin (creator of Inspector Rebus).

- You may find it helpful to learn more about the rural nature of Great Britain in the nineteenth century in order to understand the subject matter of Thomas Hardy's writing.

Further reading

- Students may be inspired to read further once introduced to some of the texts in this chapter. There are many Sherlock Holmes cases but it may be helpful to suggest *The Hound of the Baskervilles* as a starting point, because the title will be familiar to many students (and can be compared to film versions, including the series starring Benedict Cumberbatch and Martin Freeman as Holmes and Watson).

- Further Raymond Chandler novels that may appeal to students are *The Big Sleep* and *The Lady in the Lake*, both adapted by Hollywood and both part of the film noir genre, along with the masterpiece *Double Indemnity* (for which Chandler co-wrote the screenplay with the director, Billy Wilder).

- Thomas Hardy's novels are full of the rural world of the past, and any of his works will give students plenty of further evidence of his descriptive power. However, probably the best introduction to his other work is *The Distracted Preacher and Other Tales*, which will challenge students without the length of a novel (though *Tess of the d'Urbervilles* or *Far From the Madding Crowd* would perhaps be the best choices of full novels).

- On the wider theme of the description of place, students could be introduced to the travel writing of Bill Bryson, in particular *The Lost Continent* and *Notes from a Small Island*.

Planning guidelines and teaching tips

Think about how you can make the materials relevant to your students and responsive to their particular needs and learning targets. Some suggested approaches to address key areas are provided below.

- You should be aware of all students' **prior performance and targets** for the end of year or course. It may be useful to include this information (perhaps colour-coded) on a seating plan. In this way it will be easier to reseat students in different groups based on ability – whether for particular grades or a range for support.

- Think carefully about **groupings**. For instance, it may benefit students who have collaborated on a previous task, analysing a writer's use of language, to work together again to build on the former learning and develop their skills.

- Draw upon **students' wider reading** wherever possible, in particular, texts that have remained vivid in their minds due to the evocative description of place. Also encourage further reading stimulated by extracts featured in this chapter (see some recommendations overleaf), to build up their knowledge of particular literary genres and how they develop through different eras.

- Offer lots of **support** with reading texts such as *Tess of the d'Urbervilles* and *The Sign of Four*, where the lexical density of the language is more challenging due to the **historical context** of the production.

- Make sure that students are not intimidated by sharing their ideas with others and encourage them to **self- and peer-assess** – especially when dealing with imaginative writing. Students will learn from **modelling** – do not be afraid to write in front of students yourself, making mistakes and changing your mind as you work towards a more polished response.

- Some of the extracts in this chapter could create challenges for **more reluctant readers**, as well as **EAL** students. Be prepared to work with these students in one-to-one and guided group contexts to support their reading. Consider strategies to keep their interest and build their reading stamina, such as quick comprehension quizzes to add an element of competition to their reading.

- Refer to the **Grammar Reference Guide** on Kerboodle for definitions and examples of specific grammatical features covered by this chapter.

- Plan carefully for differentiation, using the **Support and Stretch activities** in the Student Book, and the additional ideas offered in the individual lesson support sections in this Teacher Companion.

Lesson focus

Preparation and resources
- Student Book 1, pages 150–151
- Kerboodle worksheets:
  - 5.1 Chronology in *Brick Lane*
  - 5.1 Imagery in *Brick Lane*

What this lesson teaches and how

This lesson further develops the skills of interpreting writers' ideas and being able to communicate those ideas concisely with the use of selected evidence. The extract, from Monica Ali's *Brick Lane*, describes the overwhelming nature of walking out into an unfamiliar physical and cultural environment. Students should focus on the imagery used to explore the sense of otherness and cultural disconnect and will also practise their ability to explain the writer's use of language and what may have been the intended effect on the reader.

Skills and objectives

The following skills and Assessment Objectives (AOs) are addressed in this lesson:
- To identify explicit ideas in texts (AO1)
- To interpret implicit ideas and select evidence (AO1)

Specification link

Paper 1, Section A, Question 1*

*Note that these same skills are transferable to non-fiction texts.

1 Brick Lane

Time travel

In preparation for the lesson, ask students to consider what it might be like to experience another period in history, if they were able to travel in time. Draw students' attention to the likelihood of an overload on their senses if they were to travel to, for example, the 14th century. Overpowering smells might be the immediate difference, as well as the sights and sounds of a different lifestyle. The activity should prepare students for understanding some aspects of Nazneen's experience as described in the source text.

Chronology in *Brick Lane*

If additional student support is required for Activity 1, distribute the worksheet 'Chronology in *Brick Lane*' on Kerboodle. Ask students to number the quotations in the order they appear in the extract. Then take feedback. Encourage students to differentiate between explicit and implicit information in the text.

Resources

Student Book 1, Activity 1 page 151
Kerboodle: 5.1 Chronology in *Brick Lane* worksheet

Support

Identifying and exploring imagery

The extract is full of imagery describing the character's overwhelming experience of London. Give out the worksheet 'Imagery in *Brick Lane*' on Kerboodle to support students' focus on imagery. This worksheet can be adapted to suit the level of support or challenge appropriate for students. More able students should be expected to develop their explanation of the imagery used.

Resources

Student Book 1, Activity 2, page 151
Kerboodle: 5.1 Imagery in *Brick Lane* worksheet

Support and stretch

Creating imagery

Set students a writing task to practise the creation of imagery in their own work, using Monica Ali's description as a model. For example, ask students to describe their journey to school, using imagery in a deliberate and focused way to create vivid pictures in the mind of the reader. All students should be able to explain their use of language and critically appraise others' ideas.

Interview with Monica Ali

As further background information, show students a clip of Monica Ali being interviewed and discussing her novels. For example, follow the weblink below. In the interview Ali describes how she wrote the novel based on her (white) mother's experience of visiting Pakistan and feeling overwhelmed by the cultural difference.

Resources

Weblink: www.tvo.org. Search for Monica Ali and select tvo.org/video/16942/monica-ali-brick-lane-and-alentjo-blue?page=1.

Lesson focus

Preparation and resources

- Student Book 1, pages 152–157
- Kerboodle worksheets:
  - 5.2 Different genres
  - 5.2 Connotations in *The Sign of Four*
  - 5.2 Unmistakably American?

What this lesson teaches and how

This lesson gives students three different texts to read and analyse and may therefore cover a number of sessions during the week. Extracts from *The Sign of Four* by Sir Arthur Conan Doyle (1890), *Farewell My Lovely* by Raymond Chandler (1940) and *Loss* by Tony Black (2010) are all examples of the crime fiction genre, whose historical context broadly matches the date of publication. The differences in subject matter, tone and style give students a rich variety of material for analysis in terms of language use for deliberate effects and the creation of setting and character.

Skills and objectives

The following skills and Assessment Objectives (AOs) are addressed in this lesson:

- To analyse how writers use language to create effects (AO2)
- To evaluate how effective writers are at creating character and settings through language (AO4)

Specification link

Paper 1, Section A, Questions 2 and 4

2 Mean streets

Different genres

To support Activity 1, distribute the worksheet 'Different genres' on Kerboodle. This worksheet can be adapted to give more or less support to students, depending on their level of need.

Resources

Student Book 1, Activity 1, page 152
Kerboodle: 5.2 Different genres worksheet

Support

Connotations in *The Sign of Four*

Activity 2 can be supported by the worksheet 'Connotations in *The Sign of Four*' on Kerboodle. Note that additional quotations have been added to the grid to increase the challenge of the task. Encourage students to explain the effects of these quotations in as much detail as they can. Invite students to feed back their ideas orally, and to discuss as a class, once the grids are complete.

Resources

Student Book 1, Activity 2, page 152
Kerboodle: 5.2 Connotations in *The Sign of Four* worksheet

Stretch

Unmistakably American?

Some students may find Activity 5 challenging if English is not their first language and/or they are not aware of the differences between some English and American terms. The worksheet 'Unmistakably American?' on Kerboodle gives some examples to get students started and asks them to give explanations or alternative terms with which they are more familiar. This can be adapted to suit the level of support required by students.

Resources

Student Book 1, Activity 5, page 155
Kerboodle: 5.2 Unmistakably American? worksheet

Support

Favourite detectives

Encourage students to discuss their favourite detectives or characters in crime fiction, drawing on examples included and beyond those featured in this lesson. They should be encouraged to explore the complexity of their chosen character and evaluate why s/he is so intriguing. This could be developed into a Spoken Language presentation.

Spoken Language opportunity

Female detectives

Ask students to consider the role of female detectives in any novels or films that they have read or seen. The character of Sarah Lockhart in Philip Pullman's *Ruby in the Smoke* and the private investigator VI Warshawski, the creation of Sara Paretksy, are two interesting examples portrayed in different historical contexts and with very different characters.

Stretch

Lesson focus

3 Rambling into danger

Preparation and resources

- Student Book 1, pages 158–159
- Kerboodle worksheets:
  - 5.3 All About Sam
  - 5.3 Structure in *God's Own Country*

What this lesson teaches and how

The aim of this lesson is to build on previously practised skills of analysis with a particular focus on structure and the presentation of character. The extract is taken from *God's Own Country* by Ross Raisin (2008), which depicts a modern rural perspective on the 'invasion' of ramblers. The later activities are quite challenging, e.g. explaining humour and its effect on the reader – and this will need some careful preparation for students to be successful and make progress in developing their skills of interpretation and explanation.

Skills and objectives

The following skills and Assessment Objectives (AOs) are addressed in this lesson:

- To analyse how writers use structure to influence readers (AO2)
- To evaluate how effective writers are at presenting characters (AO4).

Specification link

Paper 1, Section A, Question 3 and 4

Countryside v. city

In preparation for the subject matter and tone of the extract used in the lesson, ask students to think of positive and negative aspects of living in the countryside as opposed to a town or city. Encourage them to see beyond stereotypical images, such as idyllic villages and impersonal, busy cities. This could be developed into a writing task, to steer the reader towards either liking or disliking a particular setting.

All about Sam

Activity 1 moves from the relatively simple task of retrieving explicit information to asking what is understood and finally to writing a summary. The more able are asked about whether they think Sam is a hero or an anti-hero. Support is given on the worksheet 'All About Sam' on Kerboodle to help structure and understand ideas. It can be adapted to suit the needs of your students. The activity prepares students for the more demanding Activity 2.

Resources

Student Book 1, Activity 1, page 159
Kerboodle: 5.3 All about Sam worksheet

Support and stretch

What is humour?

Most students will benefit from some class discussion before tackling Activity 2. Students will clearly understand jokes and their subversive nature in society as well as their use for both ridicule and creating a comforting atmosphere through relaxation of anxieties. In this extract, humour depends on the reader understanding Sam's antipathy towards the ramblers and the possible reasons for this. Discuss examples from the extract and how to explore them effectively.

Resources

Student Book 1, Activity 2, page 159

The Great Outdoors

This is the title of a BBC sitcom which looked at how the leader of a rambling group organized rambles and how he was challenged by others. For students, the characters' appearance will be recognizable from the extract but the humour is mainly derived from the officious leader. The stereotype that Sam has developed in his head is evident in some of the available clips – most notably in the clip entitled 'A Kick up the Backside'.

Resources

Weblink: http://www.comedy.co.uk/guide/tv/the_great_outdoors/videos/

Language and structure in *God's Own Country*

Before students respond to Activity 3, ensure they read the sample commentary on the structure of the extract (in the orange panel on page 159 of *Student Book 1*) and understand the vocabulary and approach used. If students need further support in drafting their own responses, give them the worksheet 'Structure in *God's Own Country*' on Kerboodle. This worksheet can be adapted depending on the level of support required by your students.

Resources

Student Book 1, Activity 3, page 159
Kerboodle: 5.3 Structure in *God's Own Country* worksheet

Support

Lesson focus

Preparation and resources

- Student Book 1, pages 160–163
- Kerboodle worksheets:
  - 5.4 Language in *Tess of the d'Urbervilles*
  - 5.4 Narrative plan
  - 5.4 *Cold Comfort Farm*
  - 5.4 Ideas for parody

What this lesson teaches and how

This lesson focuses on an extract from *Tess of the d'Urbervilles* by Thomas Hardy, where students explore the powerful use of language and imagery to engage the reader's imagination and emotions. They are then guided through planning, writing and proofreading their own narrative, with particular emphasis on creating a strong sense of setting, character and genre.

Skills and objectives

The following skills and Assessment Objectives (AOs) are addressed in this lesson:

- To explore how writers use language and structure to create effects (AO2)
- To write a narrative piece, using a range of structural and linguistic features (AO5, AO6)

Specification links

Paper 1, Section A, Questions 2 and 3
Paper 1, Section B, Question 5

4 Tales from the dairy

Rural poor in Victorian England

Before the lesson, ask students to do some research about the lives of the poor in the countryside in Victorian England. Encourage them to find out about how traditional rural cottage industries of spinning and weaving moved into factories in towns; how more land was enclosed; how farming became increasingly mechanized, causing unemployment; the effect of poor harvests, etc. Discuss and explain that rural poverty was a key theme in many of Thomas Hardy's novels.

Exploring language

Use the worksheet 'Language in *Tess of the d'Urbervilles*' on Kerboodle to support students in responding to Activity 1. You can adapt this worksheet according to the needs of your students. As it stands, it includes more examples to consider than in the Student Book. Encourage students to explain the effects and connotations in as much detail as they can.

Resources

Student Book 1, Activity 1, page 161
Kerboodle: 5.4 Language in *Tess of the d'Urbervilles* worksheet

Stretch and Spoken Language

Engaging the reader

When responding to Activity 3, encourage students to make a plan before they start writing, to ensure that they cover features of both language and structure in their response. They should use the work done in previous activities and consider the structural effects mentioned in the Student Book. Some students might benefit from discussing their intended responses with a partner, to clarify their ideas before they start to write.

Resources

Student Book 1, Activity 3, page 162

Narrative settings

In preparation for Activity 4, different settings can be discussed and perhaps some images or clips from films can be viewed, where the settings are inextricably linked to the narrative, e.g. a post-apocalyptic city. The worksheet 'Narrative plan' on Kerboodle may be useful for students.

Resources

Student Book 1, Activity 4, page 162
Kerboodle: 5.4 Narrative plan worksheet

Support

Writing a parody

Discuss the notion of parody with higher attainers. Display the extract from *Cold Comfort Farm* on Kerboodle and talk about how it parodies the rural genre. Challenge students to write a parody of a genre of their choice. Give them the worksheet 'Ideas for parody' to get them started. Ensure that students have a firm grasp of the features of the genre they have chosen before they decide how to subvert or exaggerate them.

Resources

Kerboodle: 5.4 *Cold Comfort Farm* worksheet
Kerboodle: 5.4 Ideas for parody worksheet

Stretch

Lesson focus

Preparation and resources

- Student Book 1, pages 164–167
- Kerboodle worksheets:
  - 5.5 Spring in the city
  - 5.5 Comparing sounds
  - 5.5 Planning a comparison

What this lesson teaches and how

This lesson introduces students to a journalist's account from 1871 of what he found increasingly irritating about city life and the invasion of personal privacy. This is juxtaposed with a piece written in 2010, which deals with similar subject matter but offers a different perspective. Students will continue to build on what has been learned about writers' use of language and structure, and they will have the opportunity to write about their own perspective on the issue of noise.

Skills and objectives

The following skills and Assessment Objectives (AOs) are addressed in this lesson:
- To summarize and compare writers' ideas, with reference to the language they use (AO3)
- To write clearly and organize ideas (AO5)

Specification links

Paper 2, Section A, Question 4
Paper 2, Section B, Question 5

5 Sounds of the city

Annoying noises

In preparation for the lesson, ask students to consider what they feel to be the most annoying noise that they can do nothing to change. The discussion can be shared in small groups and then across the whole class. Categories of noises could be part of this session ranging from neighbours to siblings and parents. The key here is to set the scene for the clear tone of irritation in the first source text in the Student Book.

Finding evidence

Give students the worksheet 'Spring in the city' on Kerboodle to support Activity 1. Note that the worksheet contains additional statements to those in the Student Book, in order to extend the activity if necessary. This worksheet can be adapted for the needs of both lower and higher attaining students.

Resources

Student Book 1, Activity 1, page 165
Kerboodle: 5.5 Spring in the city worksheet

Summarize the differences

Use the worksheet 'Comparing sounds' on Kerboodle to give a framework for Activity 4. Remind students to use the information that they gather in the grid in order to write their full response. If necessary, remind them how to weave short quotations into a response. Emphasize that long quotations won't necessarily get more marks than shorter ones.

Resources

Student Book 1, Activity 4, page 166
Kerboodle: 5.5 Comparing sounds worksheet

Support

Planning a comparison

Students may find it helpful to use the worksheet 'Planning a comparison' on Kerboodle, to prepare their response to Activity 6. Remind them to find evidence from the texts (quotations) to support the points that they wish to make. Encourage them to think about how they might start and finish their response before they begin writing in detail. Prompt students to take care with their grammar, spelling and punctuation, reminding them that marks will be awarded for accuracy and clarity in their writing.

Resources

Student Book 1, Activity 6, page 167
Kerboodle: 5.5 Planning a comparison worksheet

SPAG

The sound of silence

It is a fact of modern life that many people find it difficult to cope with silence. Life is so filled with intrusive and ambient noise to which we have become accustomed that there is a fear of its absence. Ask students to consider the idea of whether we need silence at some points in our lives.

Your own perspective

Remind students that when responding to Activity 7, they should be presenting their own personal point of view about noise in the modern world. The two source texts in this lesson should have provided plenty of stimulus for students to develop their own opinions and ideas. They should not simply repeat ideas from the source texts (in the same way that in their GCSE exam, they should present their own ideas in their writing tasks, rather than reuse the ideas from the source texts provided).

Resources

Student Book 1, Activity 7, page 167

Lesson focus

Preparation and resources

- Student Book 1, pages 168–171
- Kerboodle worksheets:
  - 5.6 Evidence from texts
  - 5.6 Writing a vivid description

What this lesson teaches and how

This lesson analyses the way in which two writers describe the same place – the London landmark, Trafalgar Square. The key skills that students practise deal with the identification of features and also details learned from the texts. These skills develop into preparation for students to compare the ways in which the writers construct their views about Trafalgar Square. The final task focuses on the planning, writing and proofreading of the students' own descriptions of a place of their choice.

Skills and objectives

The following skills and Assessment Objectives (AOs) are addressed in this lesson:

- To identify and synthesize ideas from different texts (AO1)
- To explore models of language use and write a description to communicate imaginatively (AO5)

Specification links

Paper 1, Section A, Question 5
Paper 2, Section B, Questions 1 and 2

6 Trafalgar Square

Love or hate London?

Ask students to write in no more than 50 words why they love or hate London. The rationale is to make them think closely about their own opinions and also about how strongly they feel. The view could be based on a bad/good experience or just impressions of the city seen through print and visual media. Encourage the use of emotive language. Share and discuss different viewpoints.

True or false?

Activity 2 is based on a close reading of the first text. Students are given a series of statements based on information in the text and have to note them as true or false. A further activity to embed the difference between factual information and subjective viewpoints would be for students to create their own true/false quiz about their local area or school.

Resources

Student Book 1, Activity 2, page 169

Evidence from texts

To support Activities 4 and 5, give students the worksheet 'Evidence from texts' on Kerboodle. They should use this to record the different approaches that each writer takes when describing specific features of Trafalgar Square. Encourage students to make notes on the similarities and differences between the two texts. This worksheet can be adapted to suit the level of support required by students.

Resources

Student Book 1, Activities 4 and 5, page 170
Kerboodle: 5.6 Evidence from texts worksheet

The empty plinth

Explain that the fourth plinth was used for the project 'One and Other' in 2009, when individuals from the general public could use the plinth for one hour to perform, speak, recite or present anything they wished. Challenge students to develop their own spoken presentation for a specified time, for performance on the plinth.

Spoken Language opportunity

Writing a vivid description

If students need support and ideas for the writing task in Activity 7, give them the worksheet 'Writing a vivid description' on Kerboodle. This provides some possible starting points for descriptions, if students struggle to come up with their own. They could continue with one of these descriptions or decide to adopt a similar style of writing for their own description. Remind all students to check their work for spelling, punctuation and grammar, as marks will be awarded for accuracy and clarity.

Resources

Student Book 1, Activity 7, page 171
Kerboodle: 5.6 Writing a vivid description worksheet

SPAG and Support

Descriptions in note form

Ensure students understand that in the GCSE exam they will be required to write either a narrative or a description in Standard English, using full sentences. However, you could challenge higher attainers to write a description in a journal format, similar to that used by Sylvia Plath in the source text. Remind them that this style of writing has been described as 'cinematic' and 'fragmentary', but it still needs to be carefully crafted in order to create specific effects for the reader.

Stretch

Lesson focus

7 Selling the air

Preparation and resources
- Student Book 1, pages 172–173
- Kerboodle worksheets:
  - 5.7 Laurie Lee's perspective
  - 5.7 Creating an advertisement
  - 5.7 Images from town and country

What this lesson teaches and how

The text studied in this lesson is 'An Obstinate Exile' by Laurie Lee (1975), where he observes London and all its supposed charms from the perspective of the homesick latter-day rustic. He portrays London as an essentially bland and tasteless environment from which he seems to draw no enjoyment at all. Everything about his rural home is better. There is a sense of nostalgia for a lost world in this piece. Students will find plenty of evidence of the writer's emotive language and should be inspired to write some thoughtful texts of their own.

Skills and objectives

The following skills and Assessment Objectives (AOs) are addressed in this lesson:
- To analyse how writers use language to persuade readers of their perspective (AO2)
- To write imaginatively (AO5/AO6)

Specification links

Paper 1, Section B, Question 5
Paper 2, Section A, Question 3

Natural and healthy

In preparation for the subject matter of this lesson, ask students to find an advertisement from television, radio or a magazine that promotes a particular food product as 'natural' and/or 'healthy'. Manufacturers know that using these labels will attract consumers who believe that many modern foods are over-processed and use too many additives. Students can share their findings in groups or present them to the whole class.

Laurie Lee's perspective

For students who need support for Activity 1, give out the worksheet 'Laurie Lee's perspective' on Kerboodle. Encourage them to complete the grid, exploring what each quotation suggests about the author's perspective. They should then use these notes to help compose their summary.

Resources
Student Book 1, Activity 1, page 172
Kerboodle: 5.7 Laurie Lee's perspective worksheet

Support

Creating an advertisement

Develop the earlier thinking about the promotion of food products into a Spoken Language activity, for example by encouraging students to write a script for their own advertisement for an imaginary food product. Use the worksheet 'Creating an advertisement' on Kerboodle to support this task. These scripts can be performed for the rest of the class and peer-assessed.

Resources
Kerboodle: 5.7 Creating an advertisement worksheet

Spoken Language opportunity

Picture stimulus

Before tackling Activity 3, students may benefit from being shown how to plan and draft a descriptive or a narrative piece. Select an image from the 'Images from town and country' worksheet on Kerboodle (or an image of your choice), then model how you might plan your ideas for either a narrative or description. Jot down language and structure ideas, plot, vocabulary, etc. Start drafting your text, considering various options in terms of phrasing, word choice and imagery. Correct your punctuation and grammar, showing students how to hone their work.

Resources
Student Book 1, Activity 3, page 173
Kerboodle: 5.7 Images from Town and country worksheet

Sharing the best

During the drafting of the writing in response to Activity 3, students should peer-assess the language, structure and tone of drafts, and offer ideas about how to improve the effects for a reader. Collect the best uses of imagery and/or description and place them on a digital presentation so that the class can see the range of well-crafted writing being completed by themselves and their peers.

Resources
Student Book 1, Activity 3, page 173

Favourite food

A final activity, which can draw on the experience of reading the text, researching advertisements and promoting an imaginary product, is to ask students to write about their favourite food or meal. This may be a description of a particular meal, food or event linked to the meal. The aim is for the students to produce interesting, engaging descriptions.

Lesson focus

Preparation and resources
- Student Book 1, pages 174–177
- Kerboodle worksheets:
  - 5.8 Types of humour
  - 5.8 Progress check

What this lesson teaches and how

The two texts used in this chapter present very diverse portrayals of pigs (written in 2009 and 1817 respectively) and give students plenty of material with which to discuss the writers' use of humour. This is something students have practised before (in Lesson 3) and they will be able to draw on previous notes and ideas to help them develop their level of thinking and expression.

Skills and objectives

The following skills and Assessment Objectives (AOs) are addressed in this lesson:
- To analyse how writers use language, particularly humour, to create effects (AO2)
- To compare how writers present ideas and perspectives (AO3)

Specification link

Paper 2, Section A, Question 3 and 4

8 The pig issue

Finding something funny

Prepare students for thinking about humour in texts by asking them to bring in an appropriate text or extract from their own reading that they have found amusing. Remind them that humour can be quite subjective so encourage them to select something that a general audience would find funny. Students should read their choices – and give a brief explanation as to why it is amusing.

Playing with words

Discuss the humour generated by word play. There are many examples of this from television sketch shows that can be found on the Internet. The 'Four Candles' scene from *The Two Ronnies* is a particularly good example, as is the 'Mastermind' sketch.

Writing humour

Higher attaining students could attempt the difficult task of using humour in their own writing. They could describe a scene, a character or a screenplay for a comic scene. The aim is for a general audience to find the piece amusing. This should be peer-assessed and shared where appropriate. The best lines should be written on sticky notes and shared on a humour board.

Resources
Sticky notes

Stretch

Types of humour

In Activity 3 students are asked to identify the different forms of humour used in given quotations from the text. They are also asked to consider how the humour works. For students who find this too challenging, give them the worksheet 'Types of humour' on Kerboodle to assist them with this task. Note that this worksheet can be adapted to give whatever level of support is needed.

Resources
Student Book 1, Activity 3, page 176
Kerboodle: 5.8 Types of humour worksheet

Support

Progress check

Give students copies of the Progress check worksheet on Kerboodle and ask them to evaluate the progress of their skills after studying the texts in the chapter and completing the activities.

Resources
Student Book 1: Progress check, page 177
Kerboodle: 5.8 Progress check worksheet

Unit 3: Assessment

Preparation and resources

- Student Book 1, pages 178–181
- Teacher Companion, pages 107–112 [mark schemes] and 103 [chart showing links between assessment questions and exam paper questions]
- Kerboodle:
  - 5 Assessment
  - 5 Sample responses with examiner's comments for Activities 2d, 3e, 4c, 5 and 6

Assessment Objectives

All six reading and writing Assessment Objectives (AOs) are addressed in this unit (AO1, AO2, AO3, AO4, AO5, AO6).

Why do we have an assessment unit?

The final unit in each chapter of *AQA GCSE English Language Student Book 1* focuses on assessment. These units give students an opportunity to practise the skills they have developed throughout the chapter. Regular formal assessments help to monitor students' progress and assist with target-setting. Some teachers may wish to break down the assessment unit into individual activities or chunks; others may prefer to use the assessment in its entirety, to be completed under exam-type conditions where the questions are given a set timing.

Many of the activities in this unit build up to assessment questions which echo the tasks that will be set in the exam Paper 1 or Paper 2, providing early practice of responding to exam-style questions. A summary of the relationship between the assessment units and exam paper questions can be found on pages 102–103 of this Teacher Companion.

While working through Chapter 5 'Town and country', students will be developing the essential reading and writing skills for their GCSE exam. This unit assesses whether they have grasped these skills and if they can demonstrate how to employ them in an assessment situation.

What are students demonstrating?

Reading

Students will be able to:

- identify and interpret information within a text
- summarize and compare writers' ideas
- analyse how a writer uses language and structure for effect
- evaluate what a writer does to make their writing successful.

Writing

Students will be able to:

- plan, write and proofread text for a booklet giving guidance on how to manage a household and raise a family
- plan, write and proofread a piece of descriptive or narrative writing about their childhood.

How to deliver the assessment

You might wish to separate the reading and writing assessment activities into two separate lessons. Look at the questions in all of the activities and, if students are completing these under exam-type conditions, emphasize the importance of time management. A Word document version of the end of chapter assessment is available on Kerboodle which can be assigned to students.

Unit 3: Assessment continued

Understanding the assessment

If necessary, allow time to discuss what is expected in the assessment activities.

- Remind students to look carefully at the wording of the questions:

- If they are told to refer to a specific part of the source text, they must ensure that they do focus on that part, and not get distracted by the rest of the text.

- They should note key words used in the questions, such as 'summarize', 'compare', 'explain', 'language', 'structure' and 'character'. Emphasize that these words give a clear indication of what students should be focusing on, and how they should present their response.

- Warn students to check whether the question refers to just one source text or two.

- If the question contains bullet points, students should check that they do cover each point in their response and not just focus on the first one.

Support

Offer support when requested. The aim of the assessment activities is to familiarize students with working in exam-type conditions with time constraints and precise instructions. It is also to build each student's confidence in preparation for the real exam and to coach students on exam techniques as appropriate.

Marking

Activity 1 can be marked using the suggested answers on page 90. This could be done either by teachers or as peer/self-assessment. The longer, more evaluative tasks, for example the 'how' questions, can be marked using the 'Skills descriptors' in the relevant Paper 1 or Paper 2 AQA Specimen mark scheme on pages 107–112 of this Teacher Companion. Sample responses (across a range of different levels) with examiner comments for Activities 2d, 3e, 4c, 5 and 6 are available on Kerboodle.

Use the chart on page 103 of this Teacher Companion to identify which question in the end-of-chapter assessment relates to which exam paper question. If the assessment responses are produced under exam conditions, bear this in mind when marking the assessments. When marking the evaluative responses, you will want to mark using the 'best fit' principle, which means that not all points in the 'Skills descriptors' need to be demonstrated in order to achieve a mark in that level. Nor will those skills necessarily be used consistently throughout the response. Finally, you will need to make a judgement, based on your professional experience and using the AQA sample student responses (available on the AQA website www. aqa.org.uk), on points such as 'range', 'relevance' and 'accuracy' as used within the 'Skills descriptors' in the mark scheme.

AQA GCSE English Language Student Book 1 answers

Below are the answers to any largely non-subjective *Student Book 1* activities contained within this chapter.

Lesson 2 Mean streets

Activity 2

Possible connotations:

a. *'mud-coloured clouds'* – the air is filthy and almost poisonous.

b. *'the slimy pavement'* – it is hard to walk on the dirty slippery surface, suggesting danger.

c. *'the endless procession of faces'* – the city is populous and mostly anonymous.

d. *'tortuous by-streets'* – twisting, turning, muddled network, uncomfortable and unending

e. *'the coarse glare and tawdry brilliance...'* – a distasteful, brutal, superficial area of the city

Lesson 4 Tales from the dairy

Activity 1

Some suggestions:

a. *'amid the oozing fatness and warm ferments'* – this gives a sensual description of the air filled with sounds and smells which suggest growth and new life.

b. *'the rush of juices'* – this suggests that nature is flowing with new life and is linked in the passage to new feelings of love.

c. *'heavy scents'* – the smells that filled the air seemed to act like a drug, having a soporific effect on the people and the landscape – as if everything was happening more slowly than usual.

d. *'the desire of his eyes'* – Tess looks so physically attractive to Clare that he finds it impossible to do anything but act on the impulse of his desire and be drawn to her.

Lesson 5 Sounds of the city

Activity 1

Some suggestions:

a. *'the new-born day'*

b. *'jangling terrific cow-bells'*

c. *'try to sip your coffee in peace'*

d. *'throwing the refuse matter in the street, as a bouquet for your nostrils'* (irony)

Activity 4

Some suggestions:

Article 1   *war-whoop; jangling; louder yell; outscreech; discordant enough; screeching; little dog barking; 'maow'-ing in the most hellish manner*

Article 2   *unpleasant babble; intrusive noise; soundscape of calming tones; car tyres on wet bumpy asphalt; distant roar of a motorway flyover; rumble of an overground train; thud of heavy bass; baby laughing; orchestras tuning up*

Lesson 6 Trafalgar Square

Activity 1

Some suggestions:

(i)   Fact – It was laid out in the 1820s by John Nash.

(ii) Figures – dates such as 1840, 1805, 1845, 1867, 2003

(iii) Present tense – *Trafalgar Square is...*

(iv) Specialist vocabulary – *Corinthian column, pedestrianisation, plinth, refurbished*

Activity 2

a. False (he died 1805)

b. True (plus Nelson's on his column)

c. False

d. False (feeding pigeons has been banned)

e. True

f. True

g. True

h. False (art displays are temporary)

Lesson 8 The pig issue

Activity 2

Some suggestions:

Hyperbole	'Six men and a trained soldier to hunt him down!'
Farce	'The pig picked its way through the grasses and then paused, panting again, in front of the conservatory, where it deposited a sloppy, steaming stream of turds.'
Slapstick	'The Major snatched at empty air and I dived to my left, missed the animal and knocked the edge off a flower bed.'
Stereotyping	'Regiments on the flank!' cried the Major, who loved a military metaphor.'

Activity 4

a. His father was an 'independent gentleman'; his Mother was a 'spinster' called 'Dame Bess'.

b. 1st April 1816 in Avershall

c. He was placed in the care of an 'elderly man'.

d. He believes that his owner was an excellent tutor and was with him day and night. If everyone had such a tutor, the world would be better educated.

Assessment unit

Activity 1

Some suggestions:

a. He walked downstairs; cleaned boots; pumped fresh water; ate his breakfast.

b. They were close-knit; hard-working; poor; short of substantial amounts of food; always hungry; without a father.

c. It is smoky; there is a fire for cooking; the fire is poor due to low-quality coal; there are some decorative vases; a picture of their absent father stares down from the wall.

d. He writes with fondness; nostalgia; he knew it was a loving home despite the poverty.

Chapter 6: Now is the time to understand more

Chapter overview

Why are we teaching this?

Chapter 6 is designed to revise all of the reading and writing skills already practised in the earlier chapters of the Student Book. However, although new stimulus material is introduced with similar activities for students, the chapter is divided into separate units for each Assessment Objective. The aim is to consolidate students' ability to apply the skills required by the Assessment Objectives, and to increase their awareness of how and where these skills will be tested in the two final GCSE exam papers.

The writers dealt with in this chapter range from Tony Parsons, Ray Bradbury and Penelope Lively to texts written by journalists from the 19th, 20th and 21st centuries.

At the end of the chapter, full sample exam papers are available to use for internal assessment and skill development. At this point in the course, students should have the confidence to make links between the demands of the new material and the way that they have responded in previous activities. You may choose to use these sample papers as whole entities or, alternatively, to select particular questions to practise structuring specific types of answers using references and appropriate explanation.

What are the learning aims?

By the end of the chapter, students will have had the opportunity to practise and consolidate the following skills:

- Read a range of texts critically in order to identify and select evidence (AO1, AO4).
- Identify and interpret explicit and implicit ideas in texts (AO1).
- Analyse how writers have used language and structure to achieve particular effects (AO2).
- Compare how writers' ideas are conveyed across two texts (AO3).
- Write clearly and effectively, adapting tone and style for a specific form (AO5).
- Use a range of vocabulary and sentence structure for effect and with accuracy (AO6).

How will this be assessed?

- You can choose to assess some or all of the activities within each unit.
- Self- and peer-assessment should be used in order to build students' understanding of the different pitch of skill required to succeed at different levels.
- The sample papers may be used as 'mock' exams. Both Paper 1 and Paper 2 are available on Kerboodle as Word documents.
- Sample student Reading responses, across a range of Levels, are available on Kerboodle for Questions 2, 3 and 4 of both Paper 1 and Paper 2 with examiner's comments. Further marking guidance is available on the AQA website.

Lesson sequence

Below is a suggested lesson sequence, but you might choose to alter or add to it to suit your particular teaching needs. Note that the material involved in some of the units outlined may be covered over two or more teaching sessions.

Introducing the chapter

- Explain the aim of the chapter: to revise the skills practised so far in the Student Book.
- Discuss the quotation from Marie Curie.
- Explore the structure of the chapter and its focus on the reiteration of the Assessment Objectives.
- Remind students of the structure of the exam papers and which questions will be linked to which Assessment Objectives.

Assessment Objective 1 (AO1)	Assessment Objective 2 (AO2)	Assessment Objective 3 (AO3)
- Read Tony Parsons' article. - Revise the skill of identifying explicit and implicit ideas and/or information. - Interpret texts through the given activities. - Revise the skill of synthesizing and summarizing the key points in texts.	- Read the extracts from 'The Pedestrian' by Ray Bradbury. - Identify the use of language and imagery in the extracts and explore the effect on the reader. - Analyse the structure in the extracts in terms of whole text, paragraphs and at sentence level.	- Read the contemporary article by Max Davidson and the 19th-century article the 'old lady upstairs'. - Compare the viewpoints of the writers. - Explore the language used to express the viewpoints. - Explore the structure of both texts. - Write a full comparison of the two texts.
Assessment Objective 4 (AO4)	**Assessment Objectives 5 and 6 (AO5, AO6)**	**Full sample papers**
- Revise the skill of critical evaluation. - Read the extract from 'Next Term, We'll Mash You' by Penelope Lively. - Evaluate the text from the perspective of the portrayal of individual characters. - Evaluate the text with reference to the setting and its description. - Practise an exam question using ideas developed in the previous activities.	- Revise the key elements of how the two AOs are tested in the exam. - Practise planning and writing a narrative and a description (Paper 1). - Practise planning and writing to explain your point of view (Paper 2). - Practise proofreading your work, checking for accuracy with spelling and punctuation.	- These can be used as a mock exam in their entirety, or individual questions could be used to model or practise constructing responses.

Preparing to teach

Planning guidelines and teaching tips

Think about how you can make the materials relevant to your students and responsive to their particular needs and learning targets. Some suggested approaches to address key areas are provided below.

- Be prepared to **think, draft ideas and write in front of, and with, students**. Students need to be convinced that writing texts is something that everybody finds difficult – even teachers!

- Show that you can make mistakes and have to **use reference materials** to check spellings or other issues with writing. If students can be convinced that all writers are fallible and do not always get it 'right' first time, then they are more likely to experiment with ideas and language and be prepared to ask for opinions and advice.

- Read all of the texts in this section in advance and think carefully about how you can adapt the way that students interpret writers' ideas from previous activities. This can be nurtured by the encouragement of **speculative thinking** about writers' possible ideas and reasons for structuring a text in a particular way.

- Consider how to develop the level of **formality** in the way students write about their understanding of texts – including the use of literary terms in an appropriate context, rather than using words to impress.

- You should be aware of all students' **prior performance and targets** for the end of year or course. It may be useful to include this information (perhaps colour-coded) on a seating plan. In this way it will be easier to reseat students in different groups based on ability – whether for particular grades or a range for support.

- Think carefully about **groupings**. For instance, it may benefit students who have collaborated on a previous task, analysing a writer's use of language, to work together again to build on the former learning and develop their skills.

- Make sure that students are not intimidated by sharing their ideas with others and encourage them to **self- and peer-assess**.

- Refer to the **Grammar Reference Guide** on Kerboodle for definitions and examples of specific grammatical features that you feel students ought to revise.

Assessment focus

Preparation and resources
- Student Book 1, pages 183–185
- Kerboodle worksheets:
  - 6.1 Selecting information
  - 6.1 Alternative verbs

What this lesson teaches and how

In this unit, students review the skills assessed by AO1 and the areas of the exam where AO1 is the main focus (i.e. Paper 1 Question 1 and Paper 2 Questions 1 and 2). The key skill is the ability to read unseen/unfamiliar texts in order to display an understanding of what has been read. This understanding is demonstrated by the retrieval of appropriate explicit and implicit information and ideas in the text.

There is a focus on the implicit, and the idea of 'reading between the lines', in order to offer interpretations of a writer's meaning or feelings. This ability to interpret explicit and implicit information forms a basis of everything else a student needs to do in the exam, such as exploring the use of language and structure and comparing texts. The activities in this unit, which are based on analysing two newspaper articles on the subject of tattoos, give students the opportunity to practise questions which focus on AO1.

Assessment Objectives

The following Assessment Objectives (AOs) are addressed in this unit:
- To identify and interpret explicit and implicit information and ideas
- To select and synthesize evidence from different texts

Specification links

Paper 1, Section A, Question 1
Paper 2, Section A, Questions 1 and 2

Assessment Objective 1 (AO1)

Selecting information

After reading the article 'Making my skin crawl: Tattoos scream for attention' by Tony Parsons, Activity 1 asks students to identify specific points learned in lines 1–7. This is an uncomplicated and straightforward activity designed to develop students' thinking before moving on to more implicit thinking. Activity 2 (also based on the Tony Parsons text) alters the perspective of the questioning and asks students to identify which statements from a given list are true (i.e. verifiably reflecting the information they have read in the article). The worksheet 'Selecting information' on Kerboodle supports these activities.

Resources
Student Book 1: Activities 1 and 2, page 184
Kerboodle: 6.1 Selecting information worksheet

Understanding a point of view

The Student Book explains that readers move on from identifying explicit and implicit information to interpreting ideas. This also includes the use of references in support of interpretations accompanied by an appropriate and detailed explanation. Activity 3 leads students through a series of mini tasks, building up their skills to respond to a complete exam-style question in part d. Remind students that they need to quote from the text to support what they say.

Resources
Student Book 1: Activity 3, page 184

Exploring a different point of view

Students are given a second article to read, entitled 'Tattooed Royalty' (1898), which offers them a very different viewpoint. Clearly, historical context affects the opinion of the writer and this should lead to interesting discussion between students. The skills practised in AO1 so far are the basis for the ability to make connections between information and ideas in two texts (the premise of Paper 2 Question 4). Activity 4 guides students to practise the skill of summarizing.

Resources
Student Book 1: Activity 4, page 185

Using different verbs

When students write about what a writer may or may not have been feeling, they often use a narrow range of present-tense verbs. Encourage students to be thoughtful about their use of verbs and this will help them to develop the formality of their writing, as well as the clarity of their responses. Above all, ensure that students do not refer to the writer as if they were in conversation. For example, avoid 'he tells' or 'she says' as there are always more appropriate alternatives, such as 'he explains' or 'she states'. Use the worksheet 'Alternative verbs' on Kerboodle to support this point and remind students to refer to it at regular intervals throughout their course. This will also be helpful for use in the English Literature GCSE as well as the English Language GCSE.

Resources
Kerboodle: 6.1 Alternative verbs worksheet

Assessment focus

Assessment Objective 2 (AO2)

Preparation and resources

- Student Book 1, pages 186–189
- Kerboodle worksheets:
  - 6.2 Language choices
  - 6.2 Dystopian worlds: analysing language
  - 6.2 Exploring structure

What this lesson teaches and how

In this unit, students revise the skills assessed by AO2 and the areas of the exam where AO2 is the main focus. Showing an understanding of how writers use language to achieve effects and influence readers is crucial for writing successful answers to the higher scoring Question 4 in Paper 1 and Paper 2.

The activities in this unit, which are based on analysing extracts from 'The Pedestrian' by Ray Bradbury, allow students to practise responding to questions which focus on AO2 and an analysis of language and structure. They should be encouraged to explain language effects with confidence and to speculate on writers' intentions using appropriate terminology.

Assessment Objectives

The following Assessment Objective is addressed in this unit:

- To explain, comment on and analyse how writers use language and structure to achieve effects and influence readers, using linguistic terminology to support views

Specification links

Paper 1, Section A, Question 2
Paper 2, Section B, Question 3

Imagery

In Activity 1, students are asked to find a simile that creates a similar effect to the phrase 'a misty evening'. Encourage students to identify the extract: 'patterns of frosty air before him like the smoke of a cigar' and guide them towards observations about the images this creates (e.g. regular puffs of smoke, associations with men at leisure, contemplation; 'frosty air' suggests an image of crisp natural world, biting, perhaps link to 'Jack Frost', frost on windows, vegetation, something magical).

Resources
Student Book 1: Activity 1, page 187

Language choices

Activity 2 asks students to write about the connotations and effects of some given words and phrases from the extract. Students should draw on their understanding of imagery and its effects on readers, but will also need to think about the mood and atmosphere created by the writer's discrete choices of words and phrases at particular points in the narrative. The worksheet 'Language choices' on Kerboodle gives a framework for notes in response to parts a to c of this activity. Note that it covers more than one page, and can be adapted to suit the needs of students.

Resources
Student Book 1: Activity 2, page 188
Kerboodle: 6.2 Language choices worksheet

Dystopian worlds – analysing language

For further practice in analysing language used in dystopian worlds, distribute or display the resource sheet 'Dystopian worlds: analysing language' on Kerboodle. Encourage students aiming for similar targets to work together on this analysis. They might wish to make notes on the extracts. Invite feedback after students' discussion. This activity should embed students' understanding of how writers use language and imagery in texts for specific effects. It could be extended by encouraging students to write an extract themselves, using one of the same themes.

Resources
Kerboodle: 6.2 Dystopian worlds: analysing language worksheet

Exploring structure

Activity 3 asks students a series of questions dealing with Bradbury's use of structure in the extract. The worksheet 'Exploring structure' on Kerboodle gives a framework for notes in response to parts a to e of Activity 3.

Writing about structure can be challenging for students due to its broader scope dealing with the whole text, but this practice should give them confidence in approaching an analysis such as demanded in Question 3 of Full Sample Paper 1 at the end of this chapter in the Student Book.

Resources
Student Book 1: Activity 3, page 189
Kerboodle: 6.2 Exploring structure worksheet

Assessment focus

Preparation and resources

- Student Book 1, pages 190–193
- Kerboodle worksheets:
  - 6.3 Effects of different methods

What this lesson teaches and how

The ability to consider writers' ideas and texts in juxtaposition is a high-level skill in terms of GCSE. Students have to show a clear understanding of the writers' views (practised in earlier questions) before they can compare the similarities and differences in their thoughts on the same or similar subject matter. They need to be guided not only to identify the different thoughts of each writer, but to show how they may be similar or different. This should focus on the way that language is used to inform and/or persuade and also on the values and ideas of the writers.

To achieve high marks in this section of the exam (Paper 2 Question 4), students must give detailed responses and use carefully chosen references to support their views. It is also important for them to understand that the ideas in the two exam texts will not necessarily be adversarial or at odds with each other – there may be only subtle differences.

Assessment Objective

The following Assessment Objective is addressed in this lesson:

- To compare writers' ideas and perspectives, as well as how these are conveyed, across two or more texts

Specification link

Paper 2, Section A, Question 4

Assessment Objective 3 (AO3)

Considering different methods

Activity 1 asks students to find evidence to support points made in an introductory paragraph of a student response, and then to explain the effects of the methods used by writers. The worksheet 'Effects of different methods' on Kerboodle will support students in completing this activity.

If not already compiled, students could create a checklist of possible different methods that can be used by writers, in order to compare their viewpoints. They could cross-reference the different methods with where they observed them in use (either from the Student Book or other texts studied in class).

Resources
Student Book 1, Activity 1, page 192
Kerboodle: 6.3 Effects of different methods worksheet

Discussing problems with neighbours

In addition to reading the texts, it may be helpful for students to discuss the subject of 'neighbours' and share some of their positive and negative experiences. The aim is to link their own thoughts and feelings on the subject with those of the different writers. The problems discussed could be categorized into groups then compared to the situations described in the texts, leading to the consideration of whether anything has changed over time. Activity 2 asks students to interpret ideas in the texts through focused questions.

Resources
Student Book 1, Activity 2 page 192

Comparing language

Activity 3 helps students to analyse the use of idiomatic language and imagery to express ideas and opinions in the first text. The main focus is the interpretation of colloquial language and its effect on tone. In the second text the focus is on imagery and the effect of metaphorical language in particular. Clearly, AO2 deals with the subject of writers' use of language in more detail; here, it is part of the way in which writers' ideas are compared across two texts. Students could be asked to elaborate on the differences in tone as a result of the language and imagery discussed.

Resources
Student Book 1, Activity 3 page 193

Comparing structure

Some students may benefit from discussion prior to completing Activity 4. Ensure that they are aware of the main subject of each paragraph and how each plays a specific role in the whole text building up and amplifying the main point; the repetition of phrases for emphasis; the use of direct speech in each text, and the effects of the concluding sentences for final impact on the reader.

Resources
Student Book 1: Activity 4, page 193

Assessment focus

Preparation and resources
- Student Book pages 1, 194–197
- Kerboodle worksheets:
  - 6.4 Textual references
  - 6.4 Charles' mother
  - 6.4 Charles' father

What this lesson teaches and how

In this unit, students review the skills assessed by AO4 and are reminded of where these skills are relevant (Paper 1, Question 4). The key skill of 'evaluation' is described as the considered and critical judgement of a text. Students need to move beyond their own personal opinion about a subject and be able to acknowledge the strengths of a text (or texts).

Evaluation encompasses both an analysis of the content of a text and the methods used by a writer within the text to explore their ideas and perhaps persuade readers to think in a similar way (with the use of supportive textual references).

The activities focused on AO4 in this chapter are based on the reading of an extract from 'Next Term, We'll Mash You' by Penelope Lively (1978) and evaluating the presentation of characters and events.

Assessment Objective

The following Assessment Objective is addressed in this lesson:
- To evaluate texts critically and support this with appropriate textual references

Specification link

Paper 1, Section A, Question 4

Assessment Objective 4 (AO4)

The presentation of Charles

Writers can control the interpretation and sympathy of a reader in the way that a character is described in the initial parts of a narrative. The significance of just one word or phrase used by the writer can (deliberately) mislead a reader into believing that a character is going to develop in a particular way, while the rest of the text alters our initial perspective. In Activity 1 students are given specific questions about the presentation of the character-construct of Charles in order to develop their skills of evaluation.

Remind students of the importance of including textual references in their responses. Some students may find it helpful to see the resource sheet 'Textual references' on Kerboodle, which models some possible ways to incorporate textual references in a response.

Resources
Student Book 1: Activity 1, page 196
Kerboodle: 6.4 Textual references worksheet

The presentation of Charles' mother

The character-construct of Charles' mother is explored in Activity 2. There is a greater lexical complexity in dealing with the mother's 'superficiality' and this may need to be differentiated in order to engage thinking with some students (i.e. using other terms and/or comparing the way she acts with other characters from a familiar text or film).

The presentation of the mother gives students the opportunity to 'read between the lines' and look beyond the literal. This has been practiced previously and students should be able to assert their own opinions about why a writer may choose to make a character act or speak in a certain way when first introduced to readers. The worksheet 'Charles' mother' on Kerboodle gives students the opportunity of bringing together all their work done in Activity 2, in a single response.

Resources
Student Book 1: Activity 2, page 196
Kerboodle: 6.4 Charles' mother worksheet

The presentation of Charles' father

The impression a reader is given of particular characters is often closely based on their interaction with other characters in a text. Direct speech may well reveal ulterior motives and suggestions of unspoken feelings. The description of a mannerism or the adverbs used to describe the behaviour of a character can give weight to what later transpire to be 'false leads' laid down by a subtle writer. The students' impression of the father in this text will be interesting.

There will have been the initial ideas on first reading, but, after analysing both the depiction of Charles and his mother, further perspectives are opened. When students have completed Activity 3, give them the worksheet 'Charles' father' on Kerboodle. This question gives students the opportunity of bringing together all their work done in Activity 3 in a single response. Remind students to include textual references.

Resources
Student Book 1: Activity 3, page 197
Kerboodle: 6.4 Charles' father worksheet

Assessment Objective 4 (AO4)

The presentation of setting

The description of settings in narratives can often contribute equally to the development of tone and atmosphere as the depiction of character. Students will have an understanding of the power of settings, and short activities can be used to explore the immediate thoughts of most students at the words 'gloomy', 'oppressive' and 'imposing' in relation to the description of place.

In Activity 4, students focus on the description of the setting in the extract and are given referenced examples of the way the description moves from positive to negative connotations.

Resources

Student Book 1: Activity 4, page 197

Assessment focus

Preparation and resources
- Student Book 1, pages 198–201
- Kerboodle worksheets:
  - 6.5 Planning your narrative
  - 6.5 Punctuation challenge
  - 6.5 Planning your description

What this lesson teaches and how

Remind students that the writing tasks (which are assessed with AO5 and AO6) are worth equal marks to the reading questions on both papers, so the two writing tasks are worth 50% of their total GCSE marks. Before embarking on any of the activities in this unit, encourage students to review their earlier written texts and the way they were planned and drafted as well as the final assessed mark. Students should also remind themselves of any self- or peer-assessment which highlighted aspects of their writing skills that they need to improve on in order to achieve or exceed their target grade. They will then have a clear picture of how they have progressed to this point before attempting to improve their performance in the tasks set in this unit.

There are no fixed formulaic approaches to writing, because independent and imaginative thinking has to accompany any use of conventions; however, students should be practised and confident in planning, writing and proofreading their work. Remind them that technical accuracy in terms of grammar, spelling and punctuation will give clarity and cohesion to their work, and will be awarded with specific marks.

Assessment Objectives 5 and 6 (AO5, AO6)

Narrative writing (Paper 1)

Activities 1, 2 and 3 focus on how a visual stimulus (which will be included as an option in Paper 1, Question 5) can be used to elicit ideas for narrative writing. Clearly, there are no set conventions allied to using an image as the starting point for a narrative; however students should practise the thinking processes that will allow them to develop a narrative from any image given to them in an exam. Remind them that they could look at the scene from the perspective of different bystanders or imagined absent characters. The picture should suggest ideas, rather than provoke a bland, literal description.

The worksheet 'Planning your narrative' on Kerboodle will support students' planning for a narrative story. Note that this worksheet can be expanded to give students more space if required.

Resources
Student Book 1: Activities 1, 2, 3, page 199
Kerboodle: 6.5 Planning your narrative worksheet

Technical accuracy (Papers 1 and 2)

The selection of appropriate words, the structure of sentences and design of whole texts for specific purposes and effects is under the control of the writer. This is what makes all writing unique, and what makes great writing memorable and life-changing. However, to be effective, all writing has to be controlled in its structure by an appropriate choice of punctuation in order to be read in a way that reflects the writer's thinking and intentions. Clearly, too much focus on punctuation in discrete exercises will not allow the student to experiment with different effects in real writing. However, it is also true that a full range of punctuation does not have to be used in every written text in order to invest it with quality. What is important is that students have a clear understanding of the power of punctuation to make meaning clear, as well as the conventions of punctuation that cannot be ignored.

Students need to be aware that a text may only require the use of full stops and commas — and if they are deployed with skill and precision, then that text can achieve as high a mark as a piece that contains a wider range. Effective use of punctuation is a matter of what is needed for a specific purpose, not a demonstration of the use of every available aspect of punctuation.

To revise the role of punctuation in giving writing clarity and cohesion, give students the worksheet 'Punctuation challenge' on Kerboodle. Encourage students to discuss the options in pairs, before displaying a fully punctuated version (on Sheet 2). Emphasize that there are often many options when using punctuation, but students must decide which options best reflect the tone, emphasis and pace of their own writing for the reader.

Resources
Student Book 1: Activity 4, page 199
Kerboodle: 6.5 Punctuation challenge worksheet

Assessment focus

Assessment Objectives

The following skills and Assessment Objectives (AOs) are addressed in this lesson:

- To communicate clearly, effectively and imaginatively, selecting and adapting tone, style and register for different forms, purposes and audiences (AO5)
- To organize information and ideas, using structural and grammatical features to support coherence and cohesion of texts (AO5)
- To use a range of vocabulary and sentence structure for clarity, purpose and effect, with accurate spelling and punctuation (AO6)

Specification links

Paper 1, Section B, Question 5
Paper 2, Section B, Question 5

Assessment Objectives 5 and 6 (AO5, AO6)

Writing an effective description (Paper 1)

Check that students can differentiate between the form and structure of a narrative and that of a description. In some ways they can be seen as similar by students because they describe imagined experiences, places and characters involved in fictional events. However, although description is an essential element of narrative, a discretely descriptive piece of writing does not have to rely on the movement of narrative but more on the movement of a series of images and senses projected by the writer to the reader through the skilful use of language within the text.

Give students the worksheet 'Planning your description' to help them think through ideas for their writing. When students have finished their first draft, remind them to check through their work carefully for accuracy of grammar, spelling and punctuation.

Resources

Student Book 1: Activity 5, page 200
Kerboodle: 6.5 Planning your description worksheet

Explaining a point of view (Paper 2)

Stating an opinion, arguing for and against an issue and exploring how far you agree or disagree with a statement are all elements of a student's non-fiction writing throughout secondary education. As students become more proficient at adopting appropriate levels of language and relative formality, they will widen their vocabulary, develop their rhetorical skills and learn how to attempt to persuade a reader of their case.

Activities 6, 7 and 8 guide students to assemble their ideas and plan a response to the issue of banning mobile phones for under-18s. This is an excellent practice task as it will not only demand a high level of discursive and persuasive writing, but also a high level of maturity in thinking about the consequences of an action that very few students would like to contemplate in reality.

Resources

Student Book 1: Activities 6, 7 and 8, page 201

AQA GCSE English Language Student Book 1 answers

Below are the answers to any largely non-subjective *Student Book 1* activities contained within this chapter. Sample student responses to the Reading part of sample exam questions, across a range of levels, are available on Kerboodle for Questions 2, 3 and 4 of both Paper 1 and Paper 2 with examiner's comments.

Assessment Objective 1 (AO1)

Activity 1

1 Most types of people have tattoos now ('a tattooed nation').

2 Young people have tattoos ('young flesh').

3 Older people too ('wobbly, middle-aged flab')

4 Young parents ('common now on the school run')

Activity 2

The following statements are true:

- The writer dislikes tattoos.
- The writer feels that David Beckham would look better without tattoos.
- The writer thinks that David Beckham is attractive.
- The writer believes that Cheryl Cole is pretty.

Assessment Objective 2 (AO2)

Activity 1

Simile – 'like the smoke of a cigar'

The activities within the assessment units in Chapters 1 to 5 of *AQA GCSE English Language Student Book 1* all link to specific exam questions that will appear in either Paper 1 or Paper 2. The following tables show the correlation between these activities and the exam paper questions.

Note that all of these skills are transferable between fiction and non-fiction texts. In the exam, all source texts in Paper 1 will be fiction and all source texts in Paper 2 will be non-fiction.

Chapter 6 of *AQA GCSE English Language Student Book 1* does not have an assessment unit as such, but instead it has some sample papers written in the style of the AQA exam papers.

Chapter 1

Assessment activity	Assessment question	Exam paper	Exam paper question
1 AO1 Explicit and implicit ideas	a	P1	Q1
2 AO2 Structure	d	P1	Q3
3 AO2 Language	e	P1	Q2
		P2	Q3
4 AO4 Evaluation	d	P1	Q4
5 AO3 Comparison	c	P2	Q4
6 AO5/AO6 Writing		P1	Q5

Chapter 2

Assessment activity	Assessment question	Exam paper	Exam paper question
1 AO1 Explicit and implicit ideas	a	P1	Q1
2 AO2 Structure	d	P1	Q3
3 AO2 Language	e	P1	P2
		Q2	Q3
4 AO4 Evaluation	d	P1	Q4
5 AO1 Synthesis	c	P2	Q2
6 AO3 Comparison	c	P2	Q4
7 AO5/AO6 Writing		P1	Q5

Chapter 3

Assessment activity	Assessment question	Exam paper	Exam paper question
1 AO1 Explicit and implicit ideas	a	P1	Q1
2 AO2 Structure	d	P1	Q3
3 AO2 Language	d	P1	Q2
		P2	Q3
4 AO4 Evaluation	d	P1	Q4
5 AO3 Comparison	c	P2	Q4
6 AO5/AO6 Writing		P2	Q5

Chapter 4

Assessment activity	Assessment question	Exam paper	Exam paper question
1 AO1 Explicit and implicit ideas	a	P1	Q1
2 AO2 Language	d	P2	Q3
3 AO2 Structure	d	P1	Q3
4 AO4 Evaluation	d	P1	Q4
5 AO1 Synthesis		P2	Q2
6 AO3 Comparison		P2	Q4
7 AO5/AO6 Writing	a	P1	Q5
AO5/AO6 Writing	b	P2	Q5

Chapter 5

Assessment activity	Assessment question	Exam paper	Exam paper question
1 AO1 Explicit and implicit ideas	a	P1	Q1
2 AO2 Language	d	P1	Q2
		P2	Q3
3 AO2 Structure	e	P1	Q3
4 AO4 Evaluation	b	P1	Q4
AO4 Evaluation	c	P1	Q4
5 AO1 Synthesis		P2	Q2
6 AO3 Comparison		P2	Q4
7 AO5/AO6 Writing	a	P2	Q5
AO5/AO6 Writing	b	P1	Q5

Overview of exam papers

The AQA GCSE English Language course is assessed entirely with two exam papers, which students will sit at the end of their course. The following table provides a summary of these two exam papers.

Exam paper	Reading and writing questions and marks	Assessment Objectives	Timing	Marks (and % of GCSE)
Paper 1: Explorations in Creative Reading and Writing	**Section A: Reading** Exam text: • one unseen literature fiction text Exam questions and marks: • one short form question (1 × 4 marks) • two longer form questions (2 × 8 marks) • one extended question (1 × 20 marks)	**Reading:** • AO1 • AO2 • AO4	1 hour 45 minutes	Reading: 40 marks (25% GCSE) Writing: 40 marks (25% GCSE) Paper 1 total: 80 marks (50% of GCSE)
	Section B: Writing Descriptive or narrative writing Exam question and marks: • one extended writing question (24 marks for content, 16 marks for technical accuracy)	**Writing:** • AO5 • AO6		
Paper 2: Writer's Viewpoints and Perspectives	**Section A: Reading** Exam text: • one non-fiction text and one literary non-fiction text Exam questions and marks: • one short form question (1 × 4 marks) • two longer form questions (1 × 8 marks and 1 × 12 marks) • one extended question (1 × 16 marks)	**Reading:** • AO1 • AO2 • AO3	1 hour 45 minutes	Reading: 40 marks (25% GCSE) Writing: 40 marks (25% GCSE) Paper 2 total: 80 marks (50% of GCSE)
	Section B: Writing Writing to present a viewpoint Exam question and marks: • one extended writing question (24 marks for content, 16 marks for technical accuracy)	**Writing:** • AO5 • AO6		

What sorts of texts and stimulus tasks will the exam papers include?

Note that all of the texts in the English Language exam will be unseen.

Paper 1 Explorations in Creative Reading and Writing

Section A: Reading will include the following type of text:

- It will be a prose fiction literary text from either the 20th or 21st century.
- It will be an extract from a novel or a short story.
- It may be an opening, an ending or an episode within the story. It is likely to contain characters, some drama or events, description and a strong sense of atmosphere.

Section B: Writing will include a choice of two tasks:

- One task will refer to an image.
- One task will provide a written prompt.
- Both tasks will be related in some way to the source text in Section A.
- The tasks may both be descriptions, or both story narratives, or there may be one of each.

Paper 2 Writers' Viewpoints and Perspectives

Section A: Reading will include the following types of text:

- Two linked sources (both non-fiction) from different time periods and genres.
- Students will need to consider how each presents a perspective or viewpoint to influence the reader.

Section B: Writing will include just one task:

- Students will be given an opinion or statement, possibly as a quotation, but not necessarily. It will be linked to the theme or topic introduced in Section A.
- Students will need to produce a written text in response to this opinion or statement, giving their own perspective.

Assessment Objectives, mark schemes and grade descriptors

Assessment Objectives

Students' responses in the exam will be assessed according to Assessment Objectives (AOs), which have been set by Ofqual. These are the same across all GCSE English Language specifications and all exam boards.

The Assessment Objectives include both reading and writing skills, and are covered in the AQA exams as listed in the tables below.

Reading Assessment Objectives		Exam paper and question assessment coverage
AO1	• Identify and interpret explicit and implicit information and ideas.	Paper 1, Question 1 and Paper 2, Question 1
	• Select and synthesize evidence from different texts.	Paper 2, Question 2
AO2	Explain, comment on and analyse how writers use language and structure to achieve effects and influence readers, using relevant subject terminology to support their views.	Paper 1, Question 2 and Paper 1, Question 3 and Paper 2, Question 3
AO3	Compare writers' ideas and perspectives, as well as how these are conveyed, across two or more texts.	Paper 2, Question 4
AO4	Evaluate texts critically and support this with appropriate textual references.	Paper 1, Question 4

Writing Assessment Objectives		Exam paper and question assessment coverage
AO5	Communicate clearly, effectively and imaginatively, selecting and adapting tone, style and register for different forms, purposes and audiences. Organize information and ideas, using structural and grammatical features to support coherence and cohesion of texts.	Paper 1, Question 5 and Paper 2, Question 5
AO6	Candidates must use a range of vocabulary and sentence structures for clarity, purpose and effect, with accurate spelling and punctuation.	Paper 1, Question 5 and Paper 2, Question 5

The following tables show the component weightings of the Assessment Objectives in each exam paper.

Paper 1	Section A	Section B
AO1	✔ (2.5%)	
AO2	✔ (10%)	
AO3	–	
AO4	✔ (12.5%)	
AO5		✔ (15%)
AO6		✔ (10%)

Paper 1	Section A	Section B
AO1	✔ (7.5%)	
AO2	✔ (7.5%)	
AO3	✔ (10%)	
AO4	–	
AO5		✔ (15%)
AO6		✔ (10%)

Mark schemes

AQA provides mark schemes to help assess students' work. Each AO has its own mark scheme, giving guidance about the different levels that students might attain in their responses.

Teachers will find these mark schemes useful when assessing students' work during the course and in preparation for the exams. Students should also be introduced to the mark schemes, so that they are equipped to assess both their own work and that of their peers.

Knowing what the examiners will be looking for should help to inform students' own responses to the exam questions and give them a better chance of gaining higher grades.

The AQA mark schemes are outlined below for each Assessment Objective. Note that the number of marks awarded at each level sometimes varies, depending on whether the mark scheme is being applied to questions in Paper 1 or Paper 2.

AO1 mark scheme

There is no generic mark scheme in relation to the first question on each exam paper, which assesses AO1, because students' answers are either correct or incorrect.

However, on Paper 2, the second question will also be assessed against AO1, and this does have a mark scheme. See the table below.

AO1

- Identify and interpret implicit information and ideas.
- Select and synthesize evidence from different texts.

Level	Skills descriptors
Level 4 Perceptive, detailed 7–8 marks	• Shows a detailed understanding of differences between the information • Offers perceptive interpretation of both texts • Synthesizes evidence between texts • Selects a judicious range of quotations from both texts
Level 3 Clear, relevant 5–6 marks	• Shows a clear understanding of differences between the information • Begins to interpret both texts • Demonstrates clear connections between texts • Selects relevant quotations/references from both texts to support response
Level 2 Some, attempts 3–4 marks	• Identifies some differences between the information • Attempts some inference from one/both texts • Attempts to link evidence between texts • Selects some quotations/references; not always supporting (from both texts)
Level 1 Simple, limited 1–2 marks	• Shows simple awareness of difference(s) • Offers paraphrase rather than inference • Makes simple or no links between texts • Simple reference or textual details from one/both texts

AO2 mark scheme

This mark scheme is relevant to Paper 1 and Paper 2.

AO2

Explain, comment on and analyse how writers use language and structure to achieve effects and influence readers, using relevant subject terminology to support their views.

Level	Skills descriptors
Level 4 Perceptive, detailed 7–8 marks (Paper 1) 10–12 marks (Paper 2)	• Shows detailed and perceptive understanding of language/structural features • Analyses the effect of the writer's choices of language/structural features • Selects a judicious range of quotations • Uses sophisticated subject terminology accurately
Level 3 Clear, relevant 5–6 marks (Paper 1) 7–9 marks (Paper 2)	• Shows clear understanding of language/structural features • Clearly explains the effects of the writer's choice of language/structural features • Selects a range of relevant quotations • Uses subject terminology accurately
Level 2 Some, attempts 3–4 marks (Paper 1) 4–6 marks (Paper 2)	• Shows some understanding of language/structural features • Attempts to comment on the effect of language/structural features • Selects some relevant quotations • Uses some subject terminology, not always appropriately
Level 1 Simple, limited 1–2 marks (Paper 1) 1–3 marks (Paper 2)	• Shows simple awareness of language/structural features • Offers simple comment on the effect of language/structural features • Simple references or textual details • Simple mention of subject terminology

AO3 mark scheme (see opposite)

Note that AO3 is only relevant to Paper 2.

AO3

Compare writers' ideas and perspectives, as well as how these are conveyed, across two or more texts.

Level	Skills descriptors
Level 4 Detailed, perceptive 13–16 marks	• Shows a detailed understanding of the similarities and differences between the ideas and perspectives • Compares ideas and perspectives in a perceptive way • Analyses how methods are used to convey ideas and perspectives • Selects a judicious range of quotations from both texts
Level 3 Clear, relevant 9–12 marks	• Shows a clear understanding of similarities and differences between the ideas and perspectives • Compares ideas and perspectives in a clear and relevant way • Explains clearly how methods are used to convey ideas and perspectives • Selects relevant quotations as support from both texts
Level 2 Some, attempts 5–8 marks	• Identifies some similarities and differences between the ideas and perspectives • Attempts to compare ideas and perspectives • Some comment on how methods are used to convey ideas and perspectives • Selects some quotations/references, not always supporting (from one or both texts)
Level 1 Simple, limited 1–4 marks	• Simple awareness of similar and different ideas and/or perspectives • Simple cross reference of ideas and/or perspectives • Simple identification of how differences are conveyed • Simple references or textual details from one or both texts

A04 mark scheme

Note that A04 is only relevant to Paper 1.

A04

Evaluate texts critically and support this with appropriate textual references.

Level	Skills descriptors
Level 4 Perceptive, detailed 16–20 marks	• Critically evaluates the text in a detailed way • Offers examples from the text to explain views convincingly • Analyses effects of a range of the writer's choices • Selects a range of relevant quotations to validate (justify) views
Level 3 Clear, relevant 11–15 marks	• Clearly evaluates the text • Offers examples from the text to explain views clearly • Clearly explains the effect of writer's choices • Selects some relevant quotations to support views
Level 2 Some, attempts 6–10 marks	• Attempts evaluative comment on the text • Offers an example from the text to explain view(s) • Attempts to comment on writer's methods • Selects some quotations, which occasionally support views
Level 1 Simple, limited 1–5 marks	• Simple evaluative comment on the text • Offers simple example from the text which may explain view • Simple mention of writer's methods • Simple references or textual details

AO5 mark scheme

This mark scheme is relevant to Paper 1 and Paper 2.

AO5

Communicate clearly, effectively and imaginatively, selecting and adapting tone, style and register for different forms, purposes and audiences.

Level 4 19–24 marks **Content** is convincing and crafted **Organization** is structured, developed, complex and varied	**Upper Level 4** 22–24 marks	**Content** ● Communication is convincing and compelling throughout ● Tone style and register assuredly matched to purpose, form and audience; manipulative, subtle and increasingly abstract ● Extensive and ambitious vocabulary, with sustained crafting of linguistic devices **Organization** ● Highly structured and developed writing, incorporating a range of integrated and complex ideas ● Fluently linked paragraphs with seamlessly integrated discourse markers ● Varied and inventive use of structural features
	Lower Level 4 19–21 marks	**Content** ● Communication is convincing ● Tone, style and register consistently match purpose, form and audience ● Extensive vocabulary with evidence of conscious crafting of linguistic devices **Organization** ● Structured and developed writing with a range of engaging complex ideas ● Consistently coherent use of paragraphs with integrated discourse markers ● Varied and effective structural features
Level 3 13–18 marks **Content** is clear and chosen for effect **Organization** is engaging and connected	**Upper Level 3** 16–18 marks	**Content** ● Communication is consistently clear and effective ● Tone, style and register matched to purpose, form and audience ● Increasingly sophisticated vocabulary and phrasing, chosen for effect with a range of appropriate linguistic devices **Organization** ● Writing is engaging with a range of detailed connected ideas ● Coherent paragraphs with integrated discourse markers ● Effective use of structural features
		Content ● Communication is clear ● Tone, style and register generally matched to purpose, form and audience ● Vocabulary clearly chosen for effect and successful use of linguistic devices **Organization** ● Writing is engaging with a range of connected ideas ● Usually coherent paragraphs with range of discourse markers ● Usually effective use of structural features

Level 2	Lower Level 3	**Content**
7–12 marks		• Communication is mostly successful
		• Sustained attempt to match purpose, form and audience; some control of register
Content is successful and controlled		• Conscious use of vocabulary with some use of linguistic devices
		Organization
		• Increasing variety of linked and relevant ideas
		• Some use of paragraphs and some use of discourse markers
		• Some use of structural features
Organization is linked/relevant and paragraphed	13–15 marks	**Content**
		• Communicates with some success
		• Attempts to match purpose, form and audience; attempts to control register
		• Begins to vary vocabulary with some use of linguistic devices
		Organization
		• Some linked and relevant ideas
		• Attempts to write in paragraphs with some discourse markers, not always appropriate
		• Attempts to use structural features
Level 1	Upper Level 1 4–6 marks	**Content**
		• Simple success in communication of ideas
		• Simple awareness of purpose, form and audience; limited control of register
		• Simple vocabulary; simple linguistic devices
1–6 marks		**Organization**
		• One or two relevant ideas, simply linked
		• Random paragraph structure
		• Evidence of simple structural features
Content is simple	Lower Level 1 1–3 marks	**Content**
		• Communicates some meaning
		• Occasional sense of purpose, form and/or audience
Organization is simple and limited		• Simple vocabulary
		Organization
		• One or two unlinked ideas
		• No paragraphs
		• Limited or no evidence of structural features

AO6 mark scheme

This mark scheme is relevant to Paper 1 and Paper 2.

AO6

Use a range of vocabulary and sentence structures for clarity, purpose and effect, with accurate spelling and punctuation.

Level 4 13–16 marks	• Sentence demarcation is consistently secure and accurate • Wide range of punctuation is used with a high level of accuracy • Uses a full range of appropriate sentence forms for effect • Uses standard English consistently and appropriately with secure control of complex Grammatical structures • High level of accuracy in spelling, including ambitious vocabulary • Extensive and ambitious use of vocabulary
Level 3 9–12 marks	• Sentence demarcation is mostly secure and accurate • Range of punctuation is used, mostly with success • Uses a variety of sentence forms for effect • Mostly uses Standard English appropriately with mostly controlled grammatical structures • Generally accurate spelling, including complex and irregular words • Increasingly sophisticated use of vocabulary
Level 2 5–8 marks	• Sentence demarcation is usually secure • Some control of a range of punctuation • Attempts a variety of sentence forms • Some use of Standard English with some control of agreement • Some accurate spelling of more complex words • Varied use of vocabulary
Level 1 1–4 marks	• Occasional use of sentence demarcation • Some evidence of conscious punctuation • Simple range of sentence forms • Occasional use of Standard English with limited control of agreement • Accurate basic spelling • Simple use of vocabulary

Grade descriptors

Ofqual has developed new grade descriptors for the new GCSEs graded 9 to 1 in English Language. These descriptors are designed to give teachers an understanding of the likely level of performance expected in mid-point performance at grades 2, 5 and 8. Statistical predictions will be used to set grade outcomes, but these grade descriptors should be a helpful guide for teachers marking students' work.

Grade descriptors for GCSEs graded 9 to 1: English Language

1. Grade 8

1.1 Critical reading and comprehension

In relation to a range of texts, to achieve grade 8, candidates will be able to:

- summarize and critically evaluate with detailed and perceptive understanding
- understand and respond with insight to explicit and implicit meanings and viewpoints
- analyse and critically evaluate, with insight, detailed aspects of language, grammar and structure
- substantiate their understanding and opinions with illuminating references to texts and contexts
- make convincing and apt links and comparisons within and between texts

1.2 Writing

To achieve grade 8, candidates will be able to:

- communicate with impact and influence
- produce ambitious, accomplished and effectively-structured texts
- use a wide range of well-selected sentence types and structures and precise vocabulary to enhance impact
- spell, punctuate and use grammar accurately so that writing is virtually error-free

2. Grade 5

2.1 Critical reading and comprehension

In relation to a range of texts, to achieve grade 5, candidates will be able to:

- summarize and evaluate with accuracy and clear understanding
- understand and make valid responses to explicit and implicit meanings and viewpoints
- analyse and evaluate relevant aspects of language, grammar and structure
- support their understanding and opinions with apt references to texts, informed by their wider reading
- make credible links and comparisons between texts

2.2 Writing

To achieve grade 5, candidates will be able to:

- communicate effectively, sustaining the reader's interest
- produce coherent, well-structured and purposeful texts
- vary sentence types and structures and use vocabulary appropriate to purpose and effect
- spell, punctuate and use grammar accurately with occasional errors

3. Grade 2

3.1 Critical reading and comprehension

In relation to a range of texts, to achieve grade 2, candidates will be able to:

- describe and summarize with some accuracy and understanding
- respond in a straightforward way to most explicit information and viewpoints
- make some relevant comments about language and structure
- support their comments and opinions with some general references
- make straightforward links between texts

3.2 Writing

To achieve grade 2, candidates will be able to:

- communicate simply with some clarity for the reader
- produce texts with basic structures and some awareness of purpose
- show some control over sentence type and structure and use familiar vocabulary to some effect
- spell, punctuate and use grammar with limited accuracy

Spoken Language

Note that Spoken Language is assessed separately from the exam papers and will be endorsed on students' certificates. It is a compulsory requirement and you will want to integrate the teaching and assessment of Spoken Language into your course.

Suggestions for activities to develop Spoken language skills are outlined in the lesson plans for *AQA GCSE English Language Student Book 1*. See Section 3 pages 122–123 in this Teacher Companion for further details about the evaluation of students' Spoken Language.

AQA GCSE English Language Student Book 2 (ISBN 9780198340751) guides students through their preparation for each section of Paper 1 and Paper 2. It is designed for use by students in their final year of the English language course.

The teaching notes below accompany each section of *Student Book 2* and the exam papers. They include:

- guidance on what each section contains
- advice on how you might support less able students, referring to additional resources on Kerboodle
- advice on how you might challenge the most able, referring to additional resources on Kerboodle
- references to Kerboodle resources to support self- and peer-assessment.

Paper 1, Section A: Reading

Main teaching points

This paper assesses students' skill in reading a passage of 20th- or 21st-century fiction closely, in order to show how the writer uses narrative and descriptive techniques to capture the reader's interest.

At least one question on this paper is likely to require students to comment on the structure of the passage. This approach to analysing a fiction text may be less familiar to students than the others addressed in this paper, so you may wish to spend a little more time on this aspect during your initial teaching and revision.

Note that 20 marks (equivalent to half the marks for the section) are awarded to the final question in this section. This is the most challenging question and requires students to make personal judgments whilst keeping a critical distance. Many students are likely to need support to develop the most effective approach and to ensure that they allow enough time in the exam to respond fully to this question.

Supporting less able students

This paper is not tiered, and the tasks and texts in the Student Book reflect this. Consequently, less able students will need to be supported to enable them to achieve their best. The texts likely to be chosen by the examiners for this paper will generally be accessible on the surface. Where less able students are most likely to fall down is in composing their answers for the higher tariff questions.

The following approaches are likely to help these students:

- Working with a partner early on in the course, composing answers together.
- Initially, providing students with lists of useful words and phrases to link their ideas together; withdraw this support in the final term.
- Giving students the opportunity to present their answers in spoken form as presentations (this will also give them Spoken Language practice).
- Encouraging students to create personal dictionaries in which they keep new and useful vocabulary.

- Chunking up the texts so that students are only working on a short passage; they can then combine their ideas with other students who have analysed different chunks.
- Using more accessible source texts to build students' confidence, for example the extract from *The Curious Incident of the Dog in the Night-time*, on Kerboodle.
- Encouraging regular self- and peer-assessment (Progress check grids for each question, to enable students to identify their strengths and weaknesses, are available on Kerboodle).

Challenging more able students

Again, the lack of tiering may have the effect of making the questions seem rather easy for more able students. Impress on them the need to write sophisticated and thorough answers but also ensure that they don't fail to state the obvious.

The following approaches are likely to help these students:

- Selecting more challenging texts (perhaps from those studied for Literature GCSE)
- Asking students to tackle more challenging 20th- and 21st-century fiction texts (examples are available on Kerboodle with suggested activities)
- Students presenting their answers in the form of a lesson taught to the rest of the class.

Paper 1, Section B: Writing

Main teaching points

The writing section of Paper 1 is worth 40 marks (the same as for the reading section).

In this section students will write their own creative text, demonstrating their narrative (storytelling) or descriptive skills in response to a written prompt or picture.

The writing task will have a thematic link to the topic that they have read about in the reading section of this paper. However, this writing task will require them to write in a different way or from a different angle from the source text in Section A. Ensure that students are not tempted to repeat what's in the reading source in their own writing.

Remember that there will not necessarily be a choice of one descriptive task and one narrative task; they may have to choose between two descriptions or two narrative tasks, so they must be prepared for both.

Supporting less able students

Less able students are bound to feel pressured by the need to develop a piece of writing from scratch with very little support and in the restricted time frame of an exam.

The following approaches are likely to help these students:

- When they are given the choice, suggest that they write a narrative rather than a description because that gives them more structure.
- Help students to understand that narrative does not need to have a complete story arc to gain marks. They should spend time deepening and improving the craft of their writing, rather than 'finishing' the story.
- Encourage students to use the vocabulary gained from their reading in their writing.
- Plan with language in mind. Ensure that they make notes of effective words and phrases that they will then go on to use in their writing.
- Think about the effect that they want their writing to have on the reader. Encourage them to ask questions as they write such as, 'Will my reader find this interesting or exciting?'
- If they are responding to an image, ask them to imagine themselves inside the image. What might it feel like?
- Encourage them to develop the structure of their sentences to convey more information efficiently.
- Ensure that students understand the importance of technical accuracy and give themselves time to check for grammar, punctuation and spelling errors. A checklist for technical accuracy is available on Kerboodle.

Challenging more able students

Some more able writers are too nervous to take risks in the exam and play too safe in their choices of style and tone. Encourage such students to use their wider reading to develop a more adventurous preferred style, perhaps based on a favourite author.

The following approaches are likely to help these students:

- Encourage them to use their favourite authors as models, adopting their stylistic features.
- Ask them to write more than one version of a narrative or description. Each version should display distinctly different stylistic features.
- Encourage them to think about the effects that they want to have on the reader. Can they, for instance, write a description that will make their readers laugh or cry?
- Ensure that students read a wide variety of books aimed at adults, which contain examples of widely different styles and tones. Short stories are particularly recommended.

Paper 2, Section A: Reading

Main teaching points

This paper assesses students' skill in reading two linked sources from different time periods and genres in order to consider how each presents a perspective or viewpoint to influence the reader.

The paper awards a high proportion of marks to questions that require comparison. Many weaker students will need to develop the structure of their answers to ensure that they compare the texts effectively.

One of the texts will be from the 19th century. Although these will have been chosen for their likely appeal to a contemporary reader, they will still present challenges for some students in terms of their vocabulary, historical context and assumptions. Consequently, students with some knowledge of 19th-century life and culture will be at an advantage. It will also help students if they are familiar with the kinds of vocabulary that characterize texts from this period.

Supporting less able students

Because this paper includes two texts that are likely to be very different in language, tone and style, these students will need much more practice in practical aspects such as time management and ensuring that both texts are dealt with in their answers.

The following approaches are likely to help these students:

- Give them plenty of opportunity to compare texts orally, using correct terminology and comparative language. (See Kerboodle for additional texts.)

- Encourage them to read the features pages of broadsheet newspapers and articles on their websites.

- Ensure that students are aware of the areas of life that might provide fruitful comparisons between 19th-century and contemporary attitudes (for example education, gender, social policy). (See Kerboodle for additional support texts.)

- Spend time with students ensuring that they understand the differences between a modern reader's response to an old text, the original writer's 19th-century world view and a contemporary view of the same content. Many less able students will find this difficult.

- Many less able students find summarizing tricky. Give them plenty of practice by asking them to read an article and summarize it in a short time. Model the skills that you would use to do it. You might also ask them regularly to summarize their own writing (or each other's).

Challenging more able students

These students should be encouraged to make the most of the final 16-mark question of the paper. There is a danger with such students that they may get carried away 'over-answering' other questions (especially the language question) and not leave themselves enough time.

The following approaches are likely to help these students:

- Ensure that they comment on a range of features in the final question (addressing the methods used by the writers). This element of the question gives able students the opportunity to show their understanding of every aspect of the craft of writing.

- Encourage students to read a broadsheet newspaper regularly to familiarize themselves with a range of journalistic styles.

- Encourage students to read a wide range of 19th-century texts (these might include fiction too, although ensure students understand that 19th-century fiction will not appear in the English Language exam). This will help to accustom them to the vocabulary and style of the time. (See Kerboodle for additional 19th-century source texts.)

Paper 2, Section B: Writing

Main teaching points

The writing section of Paper 2 is worth 40 marks (the same as for the reading section).

In this section students will not have a choice of tasks, but they will be given a statement that expresses a point of view, and will be asked to write a response to it, giving their own point of view. What they write about will be linked to the theme of the two texts that they have read in Section A (the reading section) of the exam paper.

It's very important, therefore, that students have plenty of opportunities to develop their views on a range of topics and become skilled at supporting them with argument and evidence. Spoken Language work can really help here, especially individual presentations followed by questions 'from the floor'. Encourage listeners to be critical and articulate in their questions (a good model for this approach would be recordings of parliamentary committees when they tackle controversial topics, for example phone hacking).

You may consider devoting time in class to a topic of the week, supported by newspaper and online articles, for debate and discussion.

Students should follow this up with written essays or feature articles in which they express their opinions clearly and persuasively, taking opposing views into account.

Supporting less able students

Many less able students will find it quite difficult to identify the precise form, purpose and audience in the question, so give them plenty of practice. You may wish to model this process for them.

The following approaches are likely to help these students:

- Many less able students will not have regular access to broadsheet newspapers, so make sure you have a stock (paper or online).
- Encourage students to plan their writing with the purpose and audience always in mind. You may wish to develop a planning format that features them clearly.
- Help students to develop a range of sentence structures that can easily incorporate persuasive techniques (for example lists of three, cause and effect beginning with 'if').
- Ensure that students understand the importance of technical accuracy and give themselves time to check for grammar, punctuation and spelling errors. A proofreading advice sheet is available on Kerboodle.

Challenging more able students

Generally, these students will enjoy the challenge of this task but there is a danger that some might undersell themselves if the task isn't as exciting as they would like. Give them opportunities to write interestingly about boring topics. Set this as a challenge.

- Give students opportunities to argue extreme positions, finding ways to convince readers of views that might normally seem eccentric. This enables them to experiment with a wide range of persuasive devices, really putting them to the test. (Be wary of encouraging them to adopt a very extreme or eccentric view in responding to an exam question, however.)
- Ask students to argue the opposite of their own views. This challenges them to see topics from another viewpoint.
- You could also ask them to write in role, taking on roles that are removed from their own experience (opposite gender or different age).

Assessing student responses to sample exam papers

The final section of *AQA GCSE English Language Student Book 2* contains some sample exam papers, based on the style that students may expect to find in their AQA exams.

You may wish to ask students to tackle both papers under exam conditions as preparation close to the actual exam, or you may wish to break down the papers into their individual tasks, and ask students to respond to them as shorter tasks, either in class or as homework.

For assessment, students could be encouraged to self- or peer-assess their work, using the AQA generic mark schemes (on pages 107–112 of this Teacher Companion and on Kerboodle).

Assessment of Spoken Language

Assessment Objectives

- AO7 Demonstrate presentation skills in a formal setting
- AO8 Listen and respond appropriately to Spoken Language, including to questions and feedback to presentations
- AO9 Use spoken Standard English effectively in speeches and presentations

What is the Spoken Language task?

Students are required to complete **one** presentation in a formal context. Following their presentation they will need to respond to questions and feedback (from both/either their peers and/or teachers).

Task setting

It will be helpful if students have been given opportunities to practise some types of formal presentation in Year 9. They can then build on these Spoken Language skills throughout their GCSE course.

Many of the chapters within *AQA GCSE English Language Student Book 1* cover topics that could be used to develop into Spoken Language tasks. Opportunities are signalled in the relevant chapters of this Teacher Companion.

For the final GCSE assessment, students should have some choice in the topic for their formal presentation. Ideally, students should be speaking on a topic with which they feel confident and familiar. This knowledge can derive from personal interest or experience; it could also have been gained as a result of research in a curriculum topic of their choice. As students will need to answer questions on their presentations, secure knowledge of the topic is essential.

In order to prepare for this task, it is essential that students have had the opportunity to watch a range of presentations, including televised speeches, and discussed their strengths and weaknesses.

Task taking

When giving their presentation, students can bring prompts such as palm cards, or use visual aids. If any students are planning to prepare a visual presentation, they should receive training in the use of such presentations, and be given sufficient time to practise their delivery. Students should also be taught to cope with a range of questions.

As curriculum time at KS4 will be under considerable pressure, the modelling of formal presentations and feedback sessions is an area which schools could usefully focus on during KS3.

Use the checklist on Kerboodle to remind students of key things to remember when they are making a formal presentation. This could be adapted into an evaluation sheet for students to peer-assess each other.

Task assessment

The Spoken Language assessments will be marked by the class teacher, but will be subject to external moderation. These assessments will be separately endorsed at the end of the course and reported on the GCSE certificate. They will not, however, form part of the final GCSE English Language grade. Students will be awarded Pass, Merit or Distinction.

Use the 'Evaluation of Spoken Language presentation' on Kerboodle for guidance when assessing students' performance.

The AQA GCSE English Literature course is assessed entirely with two examination papers, which students will sit at the end of their course.

Paper 1 will assess students' understanding of:

- Shakespeare (Section A)
- the 19th-century novel (Section B).

Students will have to respond to one question on each text studied from the syllabus options. Each question will focus on a particular aspect of the text, and relate to a printed extract from the text. Students should start their response by relating to the given extract, but then widen out their response to refer to the whole text.

The grid below is a summary of Paper 1.

Exam Paper	Questions and marks	Assessment Objectives	Timing	Marks (and % of GCSE)
Paper 1: Shakespeare and the 19th-century novel	**Section A** *Shakespeare* • One answer on the studied text – based on one question related to a given extract, then write about the play as a whole. (30 marks + 4 (AO4))	• AO1 • AO2 • AO3 • AO4 (Shakespeare only)	1 hour 45 minutes	64 (40% of GCSE)
	Section B *The 19th-century novel* • One answer on the studied text – based on one question related to a given extract, then write about the novel as a whole. (30 marks)	• AO1 • AO2 • AO3		

Paper 2 will assess students' understanding of:

- modern prose or drama (Section A)
- anthology poems (Section B. Either the 'Love and relationships' or 'Power and conflict' cluster)
- unseen poetry (Section C).

In Section A, students will have to answer **one** question on their studied text (from a choice of two).

In Section B, students will have to respond to **one** comparison question that is based on one specified poem from the cluster (which will be printed in the exam paper), and one other poem from the cluster, of their own choice.

In Section C, students will have to respond to **two** questions. The first question will be based on an unseen poem that is printed in the exam paper. The second question asks students to compare the first unseen poem with another poem, that will also be printed in the exam paper.

The grid below is a summary of Paper 2.

Exam Paper	Questions and marks	Assessment Objectives	Timing	Marks (and % of GCSE)
Paper 2: **Modern text and poetry**	**Section A** *Modern prose or drama* • One answer on the studied text – from a choice of two. (30 marks + 4 (AO4))	• AO1 • AO2 • AO3 • AO4 (Modern prose and drama only)	2 hours 15 minutes	96 (60% of GCSE)
	Section B *AQA Anthology:* *Poems Past and Present* • Comparing aspects of a given poem with one other chosen from the studied section of the Anthology. (30 marks)	• AO1 • AO2 • AO3		

	Section C
	
	Unseen poetry
	
	• One question on one unseen poem.
	  (24 marks)
	• Comparing aspects of the first poem with a second unseen poem.
	  (8 marks)
		• AO1
		• AO2		

Assessment Objectives

Students' responses in the examination will be assessed according to Assessment Objectives (AOs), which have been set by Ofqual. These are the same across all GCSE English Literature specifications and all exam boards.

The GCSE English Literature Assessment Objectives can be summarized as follows:

- AO1 – is about reading, understanding and responding to texts.
- AO2 – is about learning and using technical terms to do with language.
- AO3 – is about the themes and ideas in a text, as well as when and why it was written. Context is more than background knowledge, but also an understanding of what may have influenced the writer at the time of production.
- AO4 – is all about the quality of written response in terms of sentence structure and spelling – as well its technical accuracy.

The Assessment Objectives are covered in the AQA examinations as listed in the table below.

Assessment Objectives		Exam paper and question assessment coverage
AO1	Read, understand and respond to texts. Students should be able to: • maintain a critical style and develop an informed personal response • use textual references, including quotations, to support and illustrate interpretation	Paper 1 Sections A and B Paper 2 Sections A, B and C
AO2	Analyse the **language**, form and structure used by a writer to create meanings and effects, using relevant **subject terminology** where appropriate.	Paper 1 Sections A and B Paper 2 Sections A, B and C
AO3	Show understanding of the **relationships** between **texts** and the **contexts** in which they were written. This is detailed further in the syllabus: *In teaching and assessing AO3, teachers and students can consider context in a flexible way, depending on the text itself and whichever contexts are the most relevant for that particular text. These contexts may relate to the relationship between the text and the context in which it was written. However, the contexts may also relate to the context within which the text is set: location, social structures and features, cultural contexts, and periods in time. Context, where relevant, may also apply to literary contexts such as genres, and also the contexts in which texts are engaged with by different audiences, taking the reader outside the text in order to inform understanding of the meanings being conveyed.* *Acknowledgement of the universality of a literary text is an integral part of relating to it contextually.*	Paper 1 Sections A and B Paper 2 Sections A and B
AO4	Use a range of vocabulary and sentence structures for clarity, purpose and effect, with accurate spelling and punctuation.	Paper 1 Section A Paper 2 Section A

The following table shows the component weightings of the Assessment Objectives in each examination paper.

Assessment Objectives (AOs)	Component weightings (approx. %)		Overall weighting (approx. %)
	Paper 1	Paper 2	
AO1	15	22.5	37.5
AO2	15	27.5	42.5
AO3	7.5	7.5	15
AO4	2.5	2.5	5
Overall weighting of components	40	60	100

Mark schemes

AQA provides mark schemes to help assess students' work. These mark schemes give guidance regarding the different levels that students might attain in their responses.

Teachers will find these mark schemes useful when assessing students' work during the course and in preparation for the examinations. Students should also be introduced to the mark schemes, so that they are equipped to assess both their own work and that of their peers.

Knowing what the examiners will be looking for should help to inform the students' own responses to the examination questions and give them a better chance of gaining the higher grades.

The AQA mark schemes for English Literature are outlined below. Note that more detail about how to arrive at a specific mark is given in the online mark schemes on the AQA website.

Mark	AO	Typical features
Level 6 *Convincing, critical analysis and exploration*	AO1	• Critical, exploratory, conceptualized response to task and whole text • Judicious use of precise references to support interpretation(s)
	AO2	• Analysis of writer's methods with subject terminology used judiciously • Exploration of effects of writer's methods on reader
	AO3	• Exploration of ideas/perspectives/contextual factors shown by specific, detailed links between context/text/task
Level 5 *Thoughtful, developed consideration*	AO1	• Thoughtful, developed response to task and whole text • Apt references integrated into interpretation(s)
	AO2	• Examination of writer's methods with subject terminology used effectively to support consideration of methods • Examination of effects of writer's methods on reader
	AO3	• Thoughtful consideration of ideas/perspectives/contextual factors shown by examination of detailed links between context/text/task
Level 4 *Clear understanding*	AO1	• Clear, explained response to task and whole text • Effective use of references to support explanation
	AO2	• Clear explanation of writer's methods with appropriate use of relevant subject terminology • Understanding of effects of writer's methods on reader
	AO3	• Clear understanding of ideas/perspectives/contextual factors shown by specific links between context/text/task
Level 3 *Explained, structured comments*	AO1	• Some explained response to task and whole text • References used to support a range of relevant comments
	AO2	• Explained/relevant comments on writer's methods with some relevant use of subject terminology • Identification of effects of writer's methods on reader
	AO3	• Some understanding of implicit ideas/perspectives/contextual factors shown by links between context/text/task

Mark	AO	Typical features
Level 2 *Supported, relevant comments*	AO1	• Supported response to task and text • Comments on references
	AO2	• Identification of writers' methods • Some reference to subject terminology
	AO3	• Some awareness of implicit ideas/contextual factors
Level 1 *Simple, explicit comments*	AO1	• Simple comments relevant to task and text • Reference to relevant details
	AO2	• Awareness of writer making deliberate choices • Possible reference to subject terminology
	AO3	• Simple comment on explicit ideas/contextual factors

The performance descriptors to assess AO4 are shown in the table below.

Performance descriptor	Marks awarded
High performance: In the context of the level of demand of the question, learners spell and punctuate with consistent accuracy, and consistently use vocabulary and sentence structures to achieve effective control of meaning.	4 marks
Intermediate performance: In the context of the level of demand of the question, learners spell and punctuate with considerable accuracy, and use a considerable range of vocabulary and sentence structures to achieve general control of meaning.	2–3 marks
Threshold performance: In the context of the level of demand of the question, learners spell and punctuation with reasonable accuracy, and use a reasonable range of vocabulary and sentence structures; any errors do not hinder meaning in the response.	1 mark

If students need to revise and consolidate their knowledge of grammar and punctuation, there is a range of interactive activities on Kerboodle which can be allocated to students as necessary. The GCSE SPAG Reference Guide, also on Kerboodle, is a resource for teachers who wish to refresh their own knowledge of spelling, punctuation and grammar.

Grade descriptors

Ofqual has developed new grade descriptors for the new GCSEs graded 9 to 1 in English Literature. These descriptors are designed to give teachers an understanding of the likely level of performance expected in mid-point performance at grades 2, 5 and 8. Statistical predictions will be used to set grade outcomes, but these grade descriptors should be a helpful guide for teachers marking students' work.

Grade descriptors for GCSEs graded 9 to 1: English Literature

1. Grade 8

In relation to a range of texts, to achieve grade 8, candidates will be able to:

- sustain a convincing, informed personal response to explicit and implicit meanings of texts
- sustain a perceptive critical analysis of the ways in which writers use language, form and structure
- use judicious and well-integrated textual references to develop personal responses
- show perceptive understanding of how contexts shape texts and responses to texts
- make illuminating comparisons between texts.

2. Grade 5

In relation to a range of texts, to achieve grade 5, candidates will be able to:

- develop a generally coherent and engaged response to explicit and implicit meanings of texts
- develop a clear understanding of the ways in which writers use language, form and structure
- use apt textual references to support responses
- use understanding of contexts to inform responses to texts
- make credible comparisons between texts.

3. Grade 2

In relation to a range of texts, to achieve grade 2, candidates will be able to:

- make straightforward comments about explicit meanings of texts
- describe straightforward aspects of language, form or structure
- make general references to obvious details of texts
- show awareness that texts are related to contexts
- make basic links between texts.

The *AQA GCSE English Literature Student Book* (ISBN 9780198340768) is divided into four main sections:

- Part 1 Exploring the AQA Anthology (covering both poetry clusters)
- Part 2 Unseen poems
- Part 3 Developing literature skills (with close focus on individual AOs)
- Part 4 Applying your literature skills (exam preparation).

The poetry sections (parts 1 and 2) have the most extensive coverage in the Student Book. The wide choice of texts to study for the Shakespeare plays, 19th-century novels, and modern prose and drama, means that support for these texts is inevitably more generic and less title-specific. However, the skills coverage ensures that all students, whichever individual texts they are studying, are equipped to demonstrate their skills of reading, understanding, responding and analysing literary texts.

This section of the Teacher Companion echoes the weighting in the Student Book, with the main focus on the poetry sections.

Part 1 Exploring the AQA Anthology

Part 1 covers both clusters of poetry: 'Love and relationships' and 'Power and conflict'. In both clusters, students are first introduced to the theme of the cluster, then explore the poems through a series of perspectives, which are separated into units.

The table below summarizes the sequence of units.

Units	Love and relationships Pages in Student Book	Power and conflict Pages in Student Book
1 Understanding the themes	14–17	56–59
2 Meaning and context	18–23	60–67
3 Language	24–29	68–77
4 Creating images	30–35	78–83
5 Form and structure	36–41	84–89
6 Links and connections	42–48	90–95

The following pages offer some teacher support material to accompany each unit, whichever cluster is being studied. The example activities are designed to show the type of approach and strategies that can be used effectively in the classroom. They can, of course, be adapted to suit different clusters and different students' needs.

Understanding the themes

The following skills and Assessment Objectives (AOs) are addressed in this unit:

- To read and respond to extracts from poems (AO1)
- To explore ideas and meanings (AO2)

This unit introduces the main themes and ideas shared between the poems in each cluster. Students are led to develop a personal understanding of the key themes and to consider how these may be interpreted.

Students are guided to think about the poets' presentation of themes through each poem's title, and through the language and imagery used. By the end of the unit, students should be ready to explore the poems in more detail, developing their understanding of how to look at poems from a number of perspectives.

Defining power and conflict

Linking to Activity 1 in Unit 1 in the 'Power and conflict' cluster, distribute the worksheet 'Defining power and conflict' on Kerboodle. This is designed to support students in their early thinking about the meaning of these terms. Encourage exploratory thinking and discussion. Remind them that perceptions may have changed over time, particularly if they consider other texts they may have studied, such as *Macbeth* or poetry of the First World War.

Students should share their ideas with a partner, then each pair should feed back to the rest of the class. Through this activity the class should build up a detailed picture of the way that the themes can be understood before students go on to look at the poems in more detail.

To stretch more able students, encourage them to focus on the link between power and conflict. Discuss whether power inevitably leads to conflict.

Resource

● Kerboodle 1.1 Defining power and conflict

Connotations

Ask students to consider what the titles of the poems suggest to them. Encourage exploratory thinking that links to the overall theme of the cluster. Note that the title of a poem may relate to a particular event or experience, which in turn may lead to a description of related emotions.

Ensure that students understand the term 'connotation' (an idea or feeling suggested by a word) and that they build up confidence in expressing and discussing their thoughts. You may find it helpful to look at titles of poems beyond the clusters, and to speculate on what they suggest about the theme of those poems.

This is an exercise in initial thinking, and will be useful when applied to the analysis of words and phrases within the poems themselves, as well as in their titles.

Attitudes to love

To support students in their initial thinking about the theme of love and relationships, distribute the worksheet 'Attitudes to love' on Kerboodle. Ask students to do some research to find quotations about love. You might suggest that they look at song lyrics in the first instance, but they do not have to focus solely on romantic love.

Encourage students to note a variety of quotations, including sentimental, humorous and more serious declarations. Ensure that they complete the third column, giving their view on the type of love expressed.

Resource

- Kerboodle 1.2 Attitudes to love

Using imagery to reflect themes

Draw attention to some of the images that the poets use to describe relationships in the 'Love and relationships' cluster, for example a kite, an anchor, a fishing line unreeling. Challenge students to come up with other imagery that could be used to represent different types of relationships. Draw out ideas that link with shelter, or support or perhaps even limitations or constraint. Point out that imagery can suggest qualities about a relationship that can be hard to explain in plain words.

Emphasize that the themes of love and relationships can be depicted in a wide variety of ways.

Meaning and context

The following skills and Assessment Objectives (AOs) are addressed in this unit:

- To analyse some of the ways in which meanings are created (AO2)
- To explore relationships between poems and the contexts in which they were written (AO3)

This unit guides students through ways of exploring the meaning and context of poems in each cluster. Students need to be able to offer an understanding of the main 'narrative' of each poem, the main subject matter and any particular opinion being expressed in order to explore its 'meaning'. The 'context' of a poem should be considered beyond the basic background to the poem. Context should be regarded as the key ideas presented in the poem, and their link to universal themes, as well as any social, historical or genre contexts.

Comparing contexts

In the 'Love and relationships' cluster, several poems have a number of contextual similarities. Encourage students to think in detail about these by completing the worksheet 'Comparing contexts' on Kerboodle. (The example on the worksheet is from the 'Love and relationships' cluster, but this can be adapted for the 'Power and conflict' cluster.) Ensure students understand that in the exam, they will need to make comparisons between two poems, so the more practice they get with this, the more confident they are likely to feel.

Some students may benefit from sharing ideas with a partner, before making notes on the worksheet. Check students' understanding through feedback with the whole class.

Resource

- Kerboodle 2.1 Comparing contexts

Narrative voice

Draw students' attention to the fact that context determines the subject matter, opinions and the narrative voice in a poem. To emphasize this, encourage students to construct a short poem written from the perspective of a particular 'voice'. Prepare for this activity by discussing how context can be addressed in various ways, for example:

- through a historical figure, such as a young boy in Victorian London
- through a sense of place, such as a teenager in a war-torn country
- through a social perspective, such as a single parent in poverty.

If studying the 'Love and relationships' cluster, 'Porphyria's Lover' has a very distinctive narrative voice which sets the context for the whole poem. If studying the 'Power and conflict' cluster, the narrator in 'Poppies' creates a strong context for the ideas expressed in the poem.

Setting and historical context

Some poems are set in a particular place or time, and this is an important element of their context. In the 'Power and conflict' cluster, the poems 'London', 'Ozymandias', 'The Prelude' and 'The Charge of the Light Brigade', all rely heavily on their setting to relay the main ideas. Ensure that students have sufficient historical and geographical understanding to fully interpret these poems.

After discussing these contexts, students may benefit from completing worksheets to consolidate their understanding, for example the worksheet 'London' on Kerboodle.

Resource

- Kerboodle 2.2 London

Links to universal themes

Emphasize that the way in which a poem links to universal themes is also part of its context. Model for the students how to identify first the very specific literal context of a poem (its setting, narrator, historical background, etc.) and then go on to explore how the main message of the poem widens out to relate to more general observations about universal human experiences.

Students could be encouraged to record this process through visual sketches, if that enables them to appreciate the movement from the particular to the general more fully.

Language

The following skills and Assessment Objectives (AOs) are addressed in this unit:

- To read, understand and respond to poems (AO1)
- To analyse language using suitable subject terminology (AO2)

As students develop their critical skills, the discussion of the writer's choice and use of language in a text becomes more important. Using terminology about language in a relevant way is always a key determiner between higher and lower achieving students. Unless taught otherwise, many students develop the misconception that the use of literary terminology itself will gain high marks in an examination. It won't. Knowing the correct terminology is a means to an end. Students need to use their knowledge of appropriate terminology in order to explain the precise effect of specific language on the reader.

Range of vocabulary

The first activity in this unit for the 'Love and relationships' cluster asks students to consider subtle differences between pairs of similar words. They go on to explore how swapping vocabulary in poems can shift the emphasis and mood, even if the words are similar. This activity can be extended to other words with similar meanings outside the poems; teachers can create their own pairs of words or ask students to offer more in order to emphasize the point. For example, discussion of the difference between the use and effect of the words 'love' and 'affection', would be relevant in this activity.

This approach could be applied equally effectively to the use of vocabulary in the 'Power and conflict' cluster of poems.

Diction

The term 'diction' is defined as 'the choice of words used by a writer; the arrangement of these words in particular ways to create an effect'. On Kerboodle, the worksheet 'Diction' gives students opportunity to note down their ideas about the diction of three poems (a trio from each cluster). Ensure that students comment in detail on the effects of the diction on the reader. They need to show an appreciation of how carefully poets select words and phrases and use them to create very specific effects.

Resource

● Kerboodle 3.1 Diction

The effect of rhyme, rhythm and repetition

One of the key determiners for defining poetry in some people's mind is that it contains rhyme. This is inaccurate because rhyme is not a necessary component of all poetry and too much rhyme can make a poem seem trivial and childlike. However, rhyme can play a serious role in poetry, providing a unifying quality, linking ideas and concepts, as well as providing pleasing sound patterns. Likewise, rhythm and repetition can help to give a poem pace, impact and cohesion.

To support students who need to consolidate their appreciation of sound patterns in poetry, use the worksheet 'Rhyme, rhythm and repetition' on Kerboodle.

Resource

● Kerboodle 3.2 Rhyme, rhythm and repetition

Presentation on sound patterns

Challenge more able students to create a presentation about sound patterns in poetry. This should focus on poetic devices such as alliteration, assonance, onomatopoeia, rhythm and rhyme. Students could draw examples from the cluster they are studying, or from their wider reading of poetry. Emphasize the need to show the impact of these sound patterns on the reader, for example whether they help to make something memorable, create impact, draw ideas together, help to structure the poem, etc. The simple identification of the sound patterns alone is insufficient.

Creating images

The following skills and Assessment Objectives (AOs) are addressed in this unit:

- To read and respond to extracts from poems (AO1)
- To analyse how poets use imagery to create different effects (AO2)

Imagery can be one of the most powerful aspects of poetry because the pictures created by a poet's language can encapsulate an event, a concept, a feeling or relationship very succinctly and memorably in our minds. Clearly, each reader may 'see' an image differently, depending on their life experience, but students need to be able to talk confidently about the creation of these images, and be able to explore and explain the techniques that the poet has used.

Identifying examples of imagery and using the correct terminology to describe them is only the starting point. Emphasize to students the need for them to fully explore the effects of imagery on the reader. This will, of course, include a level of personal interpretation that students should not shy away from.

Graphic images

For lower attaining students, it may be helpful to encourage them to analyse the use of imagery in some poems by actually representing them graphically. They should give consideration to colour, texture and mood, as well as actual scenes, objects or people described. They could select particular images to illustrate, or create a collage of mini-images to represent a complete poem. Ensure the students include the words from the poem (which conjure up the images verbally) in the graphic as well, and are able to explain how their pictures relate to the words.

The use of senses in imagery

Higher attaining students can look more closely at the senses underpinning poetic imagery. Encourage them to think beyond the literal and to suggest why a particular image appeals to the reader; a physical sensual connection is often the key. The worksheet 'Senses in imagery' on Kerboodle can be used to help students identify a range of images that appeal to different senses in their cluster of poems. They can also record the effects of these images on the reader.

Use the poem 'A memory of June' by Claude McKay if you wish to model how to start completing the grid. The worksheet is customizable, so you can delete all examples if you wish.

Resource

● Kerboodle 4.1 Senses in imagery

Identifying and explaining imagery

In the exam, students will be asked to choose a poem from their cluster to compare with a given poem. This means that they need to have detailed knowledge of the poems committed to memory (only one poem will be printed in the exam paper).

One way to embed some of the imagery in their minds is to ask students to note imagery from different poems onto sticky notes and display them on a board. Each student then has to take one at random and pass it on to another student, who has to explain where it is from. Other questions could be written on the back of the notes to develop the activity.

Progress check

Distribute the worksheet 'Progress check: imagery' on Kerboodle for students to complete, in order to assess their understanding of the concepts covered in this unit. This assessment could be done verbally at first, with a partner, then noted down on the worksheet. Ensure that students identify any areas of uncertainty, so that these aspects can be revisited until learning is secure.

Resource

● Kerboodle 4.2 Progress check: imagery

Form and structure

The following skills and Assessment Objectives (AOs) are addressed in this unit:

● To read and respond to extracts from poems in this cluster (AO1)

● To analyse form and structure used by writers, using suitable subject terminology (AO2)

This unit guides students through different aspects of form and structure that poets have used in their cluster of poems. The two terms are often used interchangeably, although strictly speaking the form is more about the external shape (silhouette) of a poem, and the structure is more about the internal workings (skeleton) of a poem. By the end of the unit, students should be able to identify and name technical aspects of form and structure and, just as importantly, be able to discuss their effects on the presentation and impact of the poet's ideas.

Exploring forms

To reinforce students' understanding of different poetic forms, you may wish to use poems outside the clusters. For example, Shakespeare's sonnets, Wordsworth and Coleridge's 'Lyrical Ballads', and Keats' odes provide strong examples of each of these forms. This could be extended by asking students to find their own examples of poems written in specified forms. They could then discuss them in groups, clarifying the key features which identify each form. Note, however, that many poems do not stick strictly to one form.

The worksheet 'Matching terms and definitions' on Kerboodle supports students in completing Activity 1 in the Student Book.

Resource

● Kerboodle 5.1 Matching terms and definitions

Structure and readings

Students can learn a great deal about a poet's intention in writing a text if they explore the ways in which the poem is structured as this affects meaning and the ways it can be 'read'. Revise the technical terms relating to structure, for example full rhyme, half rhyme, sight rhyme, rhyming pattern, stanza, refrain, repetition, enjambement, and encourage students to find examples of their use in poems in their cluster. Focus on what effect these structures have on the reader, how they emphasize ideas, reinforce an image or concept or guide the reader towards a certain interpretation. Encourage students to read the poems aloud, noting how the structure guides the reader in terms of emphasis, mood and delivery.

Presentation about form and structure

By the end of this unit, students should have a strong understanding of the different aspects of form and structure. Challenge higher attaining students to create a presentation in a small group, about the form and structure of a poem of their choice from the cluster. Remind them to highlight as many points as possible about the way that the form and structure of the poem guides the reader to understand the poet's thoughts and feelings.

Links and connections

The following skills and Assessment Objectives (AOs) are addressed in this unit:

Read, understand and respond to poems (AO1)

● Analyse the language, form and structure used by writers, using suitable subject terminology (AO2)

● Show understanding of the relationships between texts and the contexts in which they were written (AO3)

This unit focuses on developing the skill of comparing one poem with another, which students will be required to do in the exam. They will be provided with one poem, but then can choose another poem in the same cluster to compare it with. Students need to have a very thorough knowledge of all the poems, in order to make a suitable choice for comparison, and then be able to discuss the points of similarity and difference.

This unit encourages students to think about links in terms of theme (what is said), style (how it is said) and historical/cultural background. It draws together skills and understanding developed through previous units, for example about imagery, language, form, structure and context.

Thematic links

It is important that students understand the thematic links between the poems in their chosen cluster. In order to create a clear overview of these links, distribute the worksheet 'Thematic links' on Kerboodle and encourage students to complete the grid. Working in pairs or small groups will enable them to share and discuss ideas. Colour-coding the links will make them memorable and useful for revision. The grids can be displayed so that students can learn more from each other's perspectives.

Resource

- Kerboodle 6.1 Thematic links

Mapping links and connections

For revision, some students may benefit from depicting links between the poems in their cluster visually, using symbols and colour. Pairs could be allocated either a theme or stylistic device (such as imagery or narrative voice) and asked to create a detailed mind map, showing how this aspect links some of the poems together. The poems could be represented through symbols, for example barbed wire for 'Exposure' or a plough for 'Follower' and the links could be represented with different coloured lines. When mind maps are complete, display and discuss with the whole class.

Context research

Students are encouraged to explore their poems against the background of Romantic, Victorian and modern (20th- and 21st-century) eras. To ensure that their background knowledge is secure, ask students to research one of these three contexts in detail, and to think carefully about how this adds to their understanding of what may have affected the poets' thinking at the time of writing. Share the research as a class. Students need to be aware that this knowledge should only be used in an examination answer if it helps to explain their understanding of the poems.

Progress check

At the end of Part 1 Exploring the AQA Anthology, students are asked to evaluate their level of skills and learning in relation to the Anthology poems. You may wish students to discuss their levels of confidence with a partner, or alternatively you can give out individual worksheets: 'Progress check: Anthology' on Kerboodle and ask students to complete the self-assessment. Encourage them to identify the areas in which they are least confident, and use this to plan future activities to consolidate knowledge and understanding.

Resource

- Kerboodle 6.2 Progress check: Anthology

Part 2 Unseen poems

Students may feel uneasy at the prospect of writing about 'unseen' texts, but reassure them that they will be well equipped with the skills they need because they are exactly the same as the skills they use when writing about the Anthology poems.

The Student Book guides students through a series of units, showing them how to approach the unseen poems, looking at different aspects such as:

- meaning
- language and imagery
- form and structure
- how to compare poems
- exam preparation, for example planning responses, how to integrate quotations effectively.

Remind students of the two Assessment Objectives that will be used to measure their work in this section:

AO1 Read, understand and respond to texts. Students should be able to:

- maintain a critical style and develop an informed personal response
- use textual references, including quotations, to support and illustrate interpretation

AO2 Analyse the language, form and structure used by a writer to create meanings and effects, using relevant subject terminology where appropriate

Top tips for approaching unseen poems

Ensure that students read through the Questions and Answers section in the Student Book about the Unseen poems. This should clear up some common misconceptions. Ensure that they understand the following key points.

- They will almost certainly never have read the poems before.
- There will be two poems to read and respond to.
- The two poems will be linked by theme.
- The question based on the first poem is worth 24 marks.
- The second poem is to be compared with the first and this question is worth 8 marks.
- The section is compulsory. There is no choice – they have to answer the questions on both poems.

As students practise responding to unseen poems, encourage them to compile a checklist of Dos and Don'ts. It might start like the one opposite. Display or distribute the worksheet 'Checklist for unseen poems' on Kerboodle, for students to add to.

Do	Don't
• read the poems carefully, taking guidance from the questions and what they inform you about the subject • write about what you do understand and can explain with some confidence • use short integrated quotations from the poem to support your ideas • show that you feel there may be other interpretations but qualify this with words like 'may', 'could' or 'perhaps'.	• rush the reading – you may misread and misunderstand something important • write about the points you are not clear about as this will only highlight negative points, e.g. 'I do not understand line 2…' • make assertions about the significance or meaning of something in the poem unless you can support this with some evidence • refer to any poems other than the ones printed on the exam paper.

Differentiation and assessment

The Student Book offers additional activities to stretch the higher-attaining students and also to support the lower-attaining students. Teachers may also wish to use additional poems, to differentiate for the needs of their students. For example, students who are less confident may benefit from looking at some particularly accessible poems by Wendy Cope. Students who are more confident and need more challenge might look at some of the more complex and extensive poems by Sylvia Plath or Ted Hughes.

Encourage more able students to look carefully at the Level 5 and 6 descriptors in the mark schemes for AO1 and AO2. Discuss phrases such as 'conceptualized approach', 'exploratory thought' and 'judicious references'. Remind them of the need to use subject terminology for precision in their responses, and to be confident in supporting their detailed interpretation of the poet's ideas.

Less able students may need additional support in developing an appropriate approach to writing an analysis under the pressure of time. For example, a level of scaffolding can be offered for responses, such as planned structures for answers including an introduction and subsequent development paragraphs leading to a conclusion; sentence starters leading to a point, reference and explanation; vocabulary for describing what the poet has 'done' (for example *explains*, *shows*, *portrays*, *describes*, etc.)

Many of the activities in the Student Book can be adapted for self-, peer- and teacher-assessment. Encourage students to become familiar with the mark schemes, so that they have a clear idea of how to up-level their own responses. There is a worksheet 'Progress check: unseen poetry' on Kerboodle, that may be helpful in assessing students' overall confidence in the skills required for tackling the unseen poetry questions in the exam. Ensure any areas of uncertainty or weakness are highlighted, discussed and revisited in future teaching.

Additional unseen poems

Teachers may find it useful to have a pool of unseen poems that they can give their students at regular intervals throughout the course, so that students can track their ability to read and analyse unfamiliar texts, as the course progresses.

There are numerous websites and anthologies that provide a wide variety of excellent poems, but the following poets have produced work that has been used in examinations for both planned study and unseen analysis by different exam boards:

Seamus Heaney	Carol Ann Duffy
Sylvia Plath	Simon Armitage
Tony Harrison	U.A. Fanthorpe
John Agard	Wendy Cope
Gillian Clarke	Owen Sheers
Benjamin Zephaniah	Imtiaz Dharker
Liz Lochhead	Choman Hardi
Ted Hughes	

Poems for comparison: Missing

The two poems in the Unseen section will always be linked by a common theme. Display or distribute the worksheet 'Comparing poems: Missing' on Kerboodle. This features two poems which both focus on the loss of a loved one during war, and thoughts of life without them.

There is a similarity in tone due to the direct address of the loved soldier who is dead or missing.

The questions on the worksheets have been structured in the same way as the questions are likely to be in the exam. The first question focuses on just the first poem:

> In 'Perhaps', how does the poet present her feelings of grief and loss?

The second question asks the students to compare the two poems:

> In both 'Reported Missing' and 'Perhaps' the speakers describe feelings about a lover who is absent because of war. What are the similarities and/or differences between the ways the poets present those feelings?

Students will respond in different ways to these powerful poems but the intense feelings are vividly expressed through poignant images and the more able should identify these and explore their effectiveness.

In the table below there are some initial observations that you may wish to draw out from students. They are only a starting point for comparisons and can be added to and developed further. Remind students that they should be considering the presentation of the poets' feelings, which includes the language, imagery, structure and form, all of which are carefully chosen to relay the poets' ideas.

'Perhaps'	'Reported Missing'
<ul><li>She feels as if her life has stopped.</li><li>Her use of language, e.g. 'bereft' emphasizes the depth of her grief.</li><li>The repetition of 'Perhaps' highlights her sense of vulnerability as she cannot be sure that she will ever recover.</li><li>The capitalized 'You' shows that her love was the most important figure in her life.</li><li>There is a clear regret for something she will never experience.</li><li>Roland is described as her 'greatest joy'.</li><li>She feels that the light of the world has gone and that, for her, the sun does not shine.</li></ul>	<ul><li>She is certain that he has not died, even though this is probably the case.</li><li>The laughter of her loved one echoes in her memory and brings him to life in her mind.</li><li>She does not feel that the personified 'Death' can have taken him from her.</li><li>She disregards what others have said in sympathy and clings to the belief that he is alive.</li><li>She is certain that her heart would have stopped if he was dead, such was their closeness.</li><li>She describes his 'deep-eyed humour'.</li><li>She feels that the 'twilight hushfulness' of the world calmly waits for his return.</li></ul>

Revisiting childhood

Display or distribute the worksheet 'Comparing poems: Revisiting childhood' on Kerboodle. This contains two poems: 'Home Return' and 'Carlo's House'. These poems should be accessible to even the least confident students. The common link between the poems is that the adult narrator is reflecting on childhood and something that has been learned over time.

The questions on the worksheets have been structured in the same way as the questions are likely to be in the exam. The first question focuses on just the first poem:

In 'Home Return', how does the poet present the feelings of the man who has returned to his home village?

The second question asks students to compare the two poems:

In both 'Carlo's House' and 'Home Return' the speakers describe feelings about memories of childhood. What are the similarities and/or differences between the ways the poets present those feelings?

In the table below there are some initial observations that you may wish to draw out from students. They are only a starting point for comparisons and can be added to and developed further. Remind students that they should be considering the presentation of the poets' feelings, which includes the language, imagery, structure and form, all of which are carefully chosen to relay the poets' ideas.

'Home Return'	'Carlo's House'
• He feels like a stranger in his home village.	• He was in awe of Carlo.
• He has relative wealth compared to his past.	• He treated him like a parent and learned a lot about the simple life of the fisherman.
• He takes time to become accustomed to what was once the norm for him.	• Carlo nurtured the boy and taught him skills through play.
• We know that the place is desperately poor and always has been.	• Carlo was very skilled.
• He feels almost ashamed of his wealth.	• His house was full of interest to the boy and he loved the time he spent there.
• His feelings gradually change as he remembers more than the poverty.	• The house was precariously built but seemed part of the environment.
• He speaks to the child in himself.	• When he died the boy was very distressed.
• He starts to feel more comfortable with his surroundings and his own feelings.	• The adult can see that he lost more than just a friend when Carlo died.
• He finally feels at home.	• The poem is clearly in the past as he uses the phrase 'magnet to my childhood heart'.
• We know he is recalling the past because he uses the phrase 'self-beginning'.	• Visual imagery is used to convey colour, e.g. the 'shining silver' of the fish.
• He uses olfactory imagery to evoke the unpleasant smells of the taxis and the streets.	• There is a powerful sense of place about the house and it represents a temporary home – 'I loved that house more than my own'.
• There is a comfort in the sense of belonging – 'Warmed by the blanket of family and neighbour comfort – really home'.	

Planning for English Language and Literature GCSE

Teachers will construct their course plans in various ways depending on the needs of students. The lack of controlled assessment will enable you to develop a much more responsive and creative course than previously; however, as a consequence, you may need to set regular assessments using English Language AO focuses to ensure that you are able to track students' progress.

A number of the skills assessed in the English Language GCSE are similar to those assessed for English Literature, so it is good to consider the GCSE course as a whole. You could construct a reading course across the five (or six) terms which includes texts chosen for Literature and those that would only be relevant to Language (for example 19th-century non-fiction).

In the first year of the course, you may wish to plan your teaching around the Assessment Objectives. *AQA GCSE English Language Student Book 1* focuses on the development of skills that students need in order to meet the full range of Assessment Objectives for GCSE. You will find **medium-term plans** in the form of Lesson Overview tables at the start of every chapter in Section 1, 'Support for *AQA GCSE English Language Student Book 1*' in this Teacher Companion. These are also available on Kerboodle and can be edited to suit different requirements.

In the second year of the course, you will want to introduce students to the formats and demands of the reading and writing questions that will appear in the exam papers. *AQA GCSE English Language Student Book 2* guides students through the final year of preparation for the English Language exam. This takes the students through each section of the exam papers, giving information, advice and plenty of opportunity to hone their reading and writing skills while responding to exam-style questions.

You could use *AQA GCSE English Language Student Book 2* in a number of ways:

- Work through it paper by paper so that students understand the demands of each paper.
- Tackle the reading sections together and then move onto the writing sections.
- Work on individual Assessment Objectives by grouping together questions from both papers that tackle the same objective.

When you have drafted your initial plans, you may find it helpful to consider the following planning prompts. These relate in particular to the English Language course.

Planning prompts

1. Does our GCSE course include a wide enough range of fiction and non-fiction (including 19th-century non-fiction) to prepare students for 'unseen' pieces in the exam?

2. Do we introduce students to a study of structure in fiction early enough to enable them to reach a more sophisticated understanding?

3. Does our course encourage students to be evaluative in their responses to reading?

4. Do we teach students to summarize and synthesize the main points of non-fiction texts?

5. Are our students familiar with a range of literary terms and confident enough to use them accurately?

6. Do our students have experience of reading texts from different time periods and perspectives so that they understand the relationship between writers and the popular opinions of their times?

7. Do we encourage students to approach texts with a variety of different focuses (for example looking at structure and language in a text)?

8. Are we able to incorporate a range of spoken tasks into the course in preparation for the Spoken Language component?

9. Do students have regular opportunities to tackle 'unseen' texts independently?

10. Do we use the relevant Literature fiction set texts to support the teaching of the reading element of the Language papers?

11. Do students fully understand the importance of purpose and audience in determining the form, tone, style and structure of their writing?

12. Are students given opportunities to write at length using their planning and editing skills in a timed session?

13. Does our planning include opportunities for students to develop new vocabulary?

14. Does our planning include opportunities for students to revise and reinforce their knowledge of grammar, spelling and punctuation?

15. Is there the opportunity to introduce GCSE English Language and Literature skills in the final term of Year 9?

You might like to explore these and other planning, teaching and learning issues further in departmental meetings using CPD units available on Kerboodle: Resources and Assessment.

Assessment Objectives

There is, inevitably, an overlap of skills required for the English Language and English Literature GCSE courses. A comparison chart of the Assessment Objectives used for the Language and Literature courses is available on Kerboodle.

The table below and on pages 148–149 lists a range of approaches and activities that you could use to develop your students' skills throughout their course. Although it primarily focuses on English language AO coverage, it also gives suggestions for links with Literature texts. A digital version of this chart is also available on Kerboodle, so you can adapt it to suit the needs of your particular students.

Requirements of the AO	Suggested activities	Advice for students
AO1 Retrieving data or facts and interpreting more complex material which entails reading for inference and comprehension. Collecting material together from more than one text, summarizing and synthesizing with understanding. Key skills: • inference • comprehension • summarizing • synthesizing.	Using any of the following resources: • contemporary non-fiction • contemporary fiction (e.g. text set for Lit exam or *AQA GCSE English Language Student Book 2*) • 19th-century non-fiction 1. Ask students to work in pairs to summarize the main points of the text quickly and accurately. 2. Give students a range of statements and ask them to decide if they are true or false according to the information in the text. 3. Give students a contemporary article and a 19th-century text on the same topic (suitable texts are available on Kerboodle) and ask them to summarize and synthesize information. 4. Work with a short extract from a newspaper or magazine article, asking students to infer implicit information from it.	These are tested through 'what' questions. Always think: 'What is the writer telling the reader in this part of the text? What do we learn?' Sometimes you will have to infer the information, it will not always be explicitly stated. You will need to summarize and explain the similarities and differences between the information in texts.
AO2 A notional hierarchy – simple descriptive statements, descriptions elaborated with reference to how they work, and linkages between writing and its results. Students need to be aware of the effects of structure as well as language choice. Key skills and knowledge: • understanding writers' intentions • understanding the powers of language and structure and their effects • close analysis of text • selecting relevant supporting quotations • important literary terms.	Using any of the following resources: • contemporary non-fiction (e.g. *AQA GCSE English Language Student Book 2*) • contemporary fiction (e.g. text set for Lit exam or *AQA GCSE English Language Student Book 1*) • 19th-century non-fiction 1. Explore the structure and language in the modern novel being studied for English Literature 2. Provide students with a random selection of novels and ask them to discuss and comment on their openings. 3. Choose a page at random from any novel and ask students to investigate the language and structure.	These are tested through 'how' questions. Always think: 'How has the writer structured the texts and how has s/he selected words and phrases to influence and affect the reader?' When tackling contemporary fiction, think of the writer as a kind of film director, directing the reader to different locations and viewpoints. This is all linked to the structure of a text. Think: 'Why did the writer choose to insert dialogue there?' or 'Why has the writer moved the reader to a new location at this point?' You will need to know a range of subject terms (e.g. metaphor, simile) and use them accurately. Support your points with relevant quotations.

AO3	Using any of the following resources:	This is tested through a question that is a combination of 'what' and 'how'. You will need to identify the similarities or differences in two passages and explain how they are conveyed. Always think: 'What are the writer's views and how are they conveyed? How does this compare with another writer's view of a similar subject?'
Comparison of content and form. From identification of main similarities and differences through to sustained, detailed, evaluative and interwoven responses. Key skills and knowledge: • identifying ideas, attitudes or perspectives in two passages • comparing and contrasting • understanding the power of language and its effects • selecting relevant supporting quotations.	• contemporary non-fiction • 19th-century non-fiction 1. Give students a range of newspaper features or opinion articles and ask them to identify the writer's views. 2. Ensure that students understand how commonly held opinions might change over time (e.g. attitudes to gender or race). 3. Compare the attitudes of two writers on the same subject.	
AO4	Using the following resources:	This is tested through a question which asks both 'how' and 'how well'. Always think: 'How does the writer produce his/her effects? How successful is the writing in achieving these effects on the reader?' You will need to use evaluative language to show that you have formed a judgement. You will need to provide textual references and quotations to support your evaluation.
Expressing a personal judgement which is informed and evidenced by references to the text. Taking an overview from a critical distance. Key skills and knowledge: • understanding the writer's craft • evaluating the effectiveness of the writer's methods • critical distance • selecting relevant supporting quotations.	• any fiction text (e.g. text set for Lit exam or *AQA GCSE English Language Student Book 2*) 1. Ask students to rank passages of fiction according to their effectiveness. (This is a somewhat artificial activity but it helps students to explain their preferences.) 2. Students collect examples of passages of fiction that they rate highly (a sort of 'Desert Island Texts'). 3. Expose students to articles, TV and radio programmes in which people talk about texts that are important to them (e.g. *With Great Pleasure* on BBC R4). 4. Encourage students to form book groups to discuss their reading. 5. Any work related to works chosen for study for GCSE Lit will support this AO.	
AO5	Using the following resources:	Ensure that you understand how the purpose and audience of a piece of writing will inform its form, tone, style and register. Use your planning, drafting and editing skills to ensure that your writing is coherent and well organized.
Communicating clearly, effectively and imaginatively, selecting and adapting tone, style and register for different forms, purposes and audiences. Organizing information and ideas, using structural and grammatical features to support coherence and cohesion of texts.	• any fiction or non-fiction text (e.g. text set for Lit exam or *AQA GCSE English Language Student Book 2* reading passages) 1. Model annotating texts to show how writers achieve their effects and ask students to do the same independently. 2. Ask students to write pieces that use different content but the same purpose as the model text. 3. Adapt the text for a new purpose or audience. 4. Translate the text into a different genre (e.g. write a story based on a newspaper article).	

AO6	Using the following resources:	Continue to develop your vocabulary throughout the course and be sure to use appropriate sophisticated vocabulary in the exam.
Use a range of vocabulary and sentence structures for clarity, purpose and effect, with accurate spelling and punctuation.	• any fiction or non-fiction text (e.g. text set for Lit exam or *AQA GCSE English Language Student Book 2* reading passages)	
	1. Read and discuss the extracts as models of good writing. Encourage students to borrow vocabulary and sentence structures from them to use in their own writing.	Practise using a range of sentence structures to make your writing flow.
	2. Identify audiences and purposes in non-fiction texts and set students tasks which help them to understand how writers have crafted their writing accordingly.	Use punctuation carefully and accurately for a range of effects in your writing.
	Without using any resources, set students 'cold' writing tasks. These should have no teaching, pre-reading or discussion activities and are designed to accustom them to the exam style of writing task where they could be confronted by any topic.	Ensure that you proofread your writing as you go, rather than only at the end, in case you run out of time.

Below are sample schemes of work for English Language and English Literature. There are many ways of structuring the GCSE courses and schemes of work should be devised to suit individual school, class, teacher and student situations. If you choose to start preparing students for GCSE in Year 9, for English Language you could use Chapter 1 'Bugs' from *AQA GCSE English Language Student Book 1*. In addition to the skills, resources and assessments detailed below, you will also want to carry out Spoken Language assessments throughout the duration of the course. These sample schemes of work are also available in an editable format on Kerboodle.

English Language

Year 10	Autumn 1	Autumn 2	Spring 1	Spring 2	Summer 1	Summer 2
Skills in focus	Reading (all AOs), writing (all AOs) and opportunities for Spoken Language	Reading (all AOs), writing (all AOs) and opportunities for Spoken Language	Reading (all AOs), writing (all AOs) and opportunities for Spoken Language	Reading (all AOs), writing (all AOs) and opportunities for Spoken Language	Reading (all AOs), writing (all AOs) and opportunities for Spoken Language	Revising the reading and writing skills and AOs in the context of the exam paper questions
GCSE English Language resources	*AQA GCSE English Language Student Book 1* Chapter 1: Bugs	*AQA GCSE English Language Student Book 1* Chapter 2: Fight for freedom	*AQA GCSE English Language Student Book 1* Chapter 3: Trapped	*AQA GCSE English Language Student Book 1* Chapter 4: All in the mind	*AQA GCSE English Language Student Book 1* Chapter 5: Town and country	*AQA GCSE English Language Student Book 1* Chapter 6: Now is the time to understand more
Assessment opportunities	Unit 2 Progress check Unit 3 Assessment	Unit 3 Progress check Unit 4 Assessment	Unit 2 Progress check Unit 3 Assessment	Unit 2 Progress check Unit 3 Assessment	Unit 2 Progress check Unit 3 Assessment	Sample exam papers (for mock exams)

Year 11	Autumn 1	Autumn 2	Spring 1	Spring 2	Summer 1	Summer 2
Skills in focus	Reading and exploring fiction	Writing imaginatively and creatively	Reading non-fiction for information and viewpoint	Writing to present a viewpoint or perspective	Revision	Exams
GCSE English Language resources	*AQA GCSE English Language Student Book 2* Paper 1 Explorations in creative reading and writing	*AQA GCSE English Language Student Book 2* Paper 1 Explorations in creative reading and writing	*AQA GCSE English Language Student Book 2* Paper 2 Writers' viewpoints and perspectives	*AQA GCSE English Language Student Book 2* Paper 2 Writers' viewpoints and perspectives	*AQA GCSE English Language Student Book 2* Sample exam papers	Exams
Assessment opportunities	Self- and peer-assessment activities End-of-chapter progress checks	Self- and peer-assessment in every chapter	Self- and peer-assessment activities End-of-chapter progress checks	Self- and peer-assessment in every chapter	Sample exam papers	Exams

English Literature

For English Literature, during the course you need to prepare students for:

- one Shakespeare play
- one 19th-century novel
- either one modern novel or one modern play
- the poetry anthology
- unseen poetry.

You will want to devise a scheme of work that suits your school, staff and students. You may also wish to consider where skills or content overlap with English Language. For example:

- Responding to unseen 20th/21st-century fiction texts in English Language could be taught alongside modern prose/drama.
- When teaching the 19th-century novel in English Literature, you could introduce some related non-fiction texts from the same period to help prepare for English Language.

The following sample scheme of work is just one way of dividing up the content of the specification:

Year	Autumn 1	Autumn 2	Spring 1	Spring 2	Summer 1	Summer 2
Year 10	Shakespeare and poetry anthology	Shakespeare and poetry anthology	Modern prose/drama	Modern prose/drama	Unseen poetry	Mock exam
Year 11	19th-century novel	19th-century novel	Revision Mock exam	Revision	Revision	Exams

Year 9

You will also want to consider when and how to start preparing students for GCSE at KS3. Approaching KS3 teaching through themes could be a beneficial way to prepare students for the new GCSE English Language qualification during Years 7, 8 and 9. You might like to make use of the Oxford University Press *Ignite English* resources for this purpose.

In Year 9, you might choose to start the beginning of the GCSE course by looking at:

- some writing by one of the English Literature set text authors
- collections of fiction and non-fiction texts and extracts across the 19th, 20th and 21st centuries, particularly focusing on 19th-century non-fiction texts (Oxford University Press has a *Rollercoaster* collection of 19th-century fiction and non-fiction texts that might prove helpful, with a free online teacher resource)
- developing reading and writing skills that satisfy the KS3 National Curriculum but that also help start to prepare students for GCSE English Language carry out one or more (mock) Spoken Language assessments.

This does not necessarily mean that Year 9 is the beginning of GCSE assessment preparation, but it starts the process of narrowing the focus onto the skills and content of the GCSE specifications before embarking on in-depth question-specific assessment preparation later in the GCSE course.

Grading the New GCSEs in 2017   Ofqual

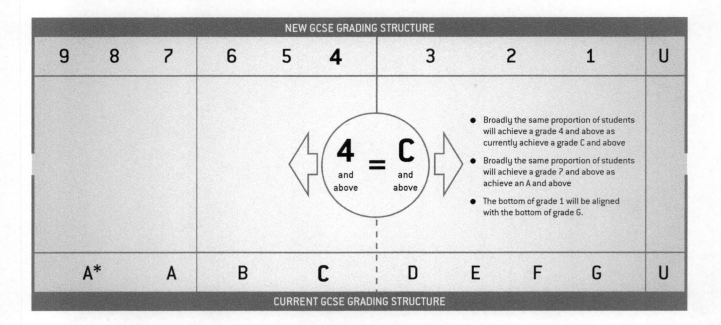

NEW GCSE GRADING STRUCTURE											
9	8	7	6	5	**4**	3	2	1	U

4 and above = C and above

- Broadly the same proportion of students will achieve a grade 4 and above as currently achieve a grade C and above
- Broadly the same proportion of students will achieve a grade 7 and above as achieve an A and above
- The bottom of grade 1 will be aligned with the bottom of grade G.

| A* | A | B | C | D | E | F | G | U |

CURRENT GCSE GRADING STRUCTURE